BRAVE WOMEN AT WORK

Stories of Resilience

BRAVE WOMEN AT WORK

Stories of Resilience

JENNIFER PESTIKAS

Managing Editor
HOPE MUELLER

- Yalonda Brown
- Kim Ellet
- Georgie Komeiner
- Shelia Higgs Burkhalter
- Betsy Gornet
- Trisha Tayan

Hunter Street Press

Brave Women at Work
Stories of Resilience

Copyright ©2022 by Hope Mueller
All rights reserved.

No part of this publication may be reproduced, stored in a retrieval system, or transmitted in any form or by any means—electronic, mechanical, photocopy, recording, or any other—without the prior permission of the author.

ISBN: 979-8-218-02692-9 (hardcover)
ISBN: 979-8-218-02691-2 (ebook)

Printed in the United States of America

PRAISE FOR
BRAVE WOMEN AT WORK: STORIES OF RESILIENCE

"These eight stories detail choices we make on our individual journeys. While the choices are always ours, these eight women provide direct and powerful insight that inspire us toward more honest choices. Blunt, smart and informative, the best moments within will challenge what you think you know about facing the road ahead."

—**G. Fiscus**, Owner/Managing Partner

"Oh, my goodness! It was amazing. I am inspired. I might be crying, but these are tears of joy and admiration. Once I started reading *Brave Women at Work*, I couldn't put it down. I am so moved by the authentic stories and lessons shared in this book."

—**A. Higgs**, MBA, MA, Corporate Director of Health

"Although the book is titled *Brave Women at Work*, the subtitle 'Stories of Resilience' was the treasure gained as I read each section of the book. This collection of each author's intimately shared life story was powerful and led me to reflect on life's joys, self-love, relationships, and grace for others as well as for myself. An inspirational and compelling read!"

—L. King

"The underlying/recurring resilience-focused theme resonates with me. The book title says it all: Each authors is a brave women who, when confronted with tough challenges or problems, demonstrated remarkable resilience."

—J. Kho

"This book not only focuses on stories of resilience but of triumphs! These women excelled despite the obstacles they each faced."

—J. Milewski

"This book eloquently gives a voice to those of us who've had to persevere and survive in silence. The women in this book challenge readers to be the light in the tunnel instead of waiting for light at the end of it."

—M. Caldwell,
Host of Miguel's Black Coffee, the podcast

"*Brave Women At Work* is a massive breath of fresh air for working women, and modern women in general. I can feel my own experience as a woman navigating her career options in the face of personal challenges, ones I've often felt I could never speak about, reflected in all of these stories. They are told with a depth and vulnerability that goes beyond the usual mediums through which I frequently encounter female "success" stories (social media, newspapers, women's magazines, TV news shows). The relief in me is deep and visceral as these women share openly, in their own voices, about the mental, emotional, and physical health challenges, cultural biases, gutting losses, and other obstacles they have faced and continued to navigate today. I love knowing I can open this book any time and find grounded guidance and inspiration from women who have lived through the process of personal reinvention and transformation, figured out what they wanted, and have gone after it in life. I look forward to gifting this book to my college-aged niece and all my girlfriends, so that we can all move from a place of not just surviving our experiences but thriving as professional women who can offer grace and support to each other as we share our stories."

—**A. McCampbell**, Office Manager NLP Marin

"Wonderful glimpses into women who have not only persevered but have lived lives of impact. Powerful. Motivating. Relatable. A must read!"

—**J. Mitchell**, Financial Advisor

"The experiences shared in *Brave Women at Work* are a helpful reminder that bravery is a practice cultivated by courage, authenticity, and self-preservation - all of which are needed in contemporary workplaces that prize wisdom, diversity, learning, and well-being of formal and informal leaders. If you're seeking guideposts to strengthen your voice in your chosen profession or in your life, you'll find value in this book."

—**K.D. Kendrick**, MSLS, Owner, Kendrick Consulting & Communications, LLC

"Resilience- to bend without breaking. These extraordinary women share stories that we all recognize. Either from our own story or of someone we know. Very helpful to remind us we are not alone."

—**D. Stovall**, www.Debbiestovall.com

"Even if you do not face the specific challenges faced by these authors, their advice is helpful to anyone serving in a leadership role. Moreover, their stories help us better understand what people in our organizations are facing in their lives and that understanding is valuable to all of us who are trying to improve our places of work."

—**D. Mahony**, Ph.D., University President

"At some point in our lives, we will all struggle with something. When life hits the fan and we aren't sure how we are going to manage it, the stories in this book will help us see that we are not alone and give us hope. I highly recommend you read this, even if you're not struggling now, it will help when you do!"

—**Janet Fouts**, Human Potential Facilitator, CEO of Tatu Digital Media, and Author of *Microdosed Mindfulness*

"There are many components of this book that elevate it well over significant and important. The chapters reflect the journeys of the women who rather than bend to the pressures of life, stand up to face them straight on. It is an inspiring read for anybody, and I absolutely recommend it."

—**T. Porch**, Investment Assistant

"There are many books on the strategies and tactics to be successful at work, but they often leave out how intertwined our personal lives are with professional success. The stories from the impressive group of authors of Brave Women at Work show us how a diverse group of women have handled personal and professional challenges and tragedies, and used lessons learned to create careers of achievement and purpose. You will be inspired by the book to reflect on your own career and life journey and how to define your own path."

—**P. Chuang**, Healthcare Executive

"Inspiring. Resilient. Intriguing. Brave Women at Work will open your eyes to personal stories about change and finding yourself."

—**B. Lemon**, Teacher

"Each contributing author in this book shares a story of significant challenge that emerge in various ways in their lives. They explore the poignant unveiling of their secret struggles and the power of tenacity and resilience."

—**G. Davis**, Ret Chief Financial Officer

"The voices collected here tell of more than pain, heartache, and hardship. They also sing of grit, determination, and triumph. These stories are told by real people who have pushed through and accomplished far beyond the expectations of others because they transformed feelings of disappointment, failure and grief into the bright and powerful energy of resilience.

This inspiring anthology would be helpful to anyone who feels the odds stacked against them and who wants to get unstuck from the inertia of victimhood."

—**J. Shropshire**, Ret Business Consultant

"These women are bravely sharing stories that can benefit us all. They validate our experiences and the power that can come from listening to our inner whispers and taking bold action despite the many ways society conditions us not to."

—**J. Hanserd**, Principal Hanserd Health Solutions

"Shelia Higgs Burkhalter thank you for listening to that still, small powerful siren that gave you permission to be authentic. God often hides the overall mission so that we won't shrink back."

—**M. Higgs**, MBA, MRED, PMP, Real Estate Professional

"The first chapter drew me in like a good movie. Shelia Higgs Burkhalter has reached heights others can only dream of. But now we know what's possible for us after hearing her story."

—**S. Decatur**, Supervisor/Pharmacy Technician

"This is a great read with real stories of fear, danger and pain. Each Brave Woman pushed through work and life challenges with unique courage and tenacity. I will share widely and pass on these stunning messages in the hopes that others will find the freedom Shelia Higgs Burkhalter describes when you trust your intuition and enjoy the victories that authenticity provides."

—**T. Bump**, Ph.D., Vice President
University Relations & Student Affairs

"First, Only, Different no longer equates to loneliness. S.Higgs Burkhalter shares relatable experiences with powerful lessons about knowledge of self while leading during challenging times, courage to speak when vulnerable, and ways to "walk boldly into [your] freedom." Priceless!"

—**G. Cole-Avent**, Ph.D., Associate Vice President

"As an expert on developing a positive mindset to enjoy more work-life balance, I'm always looking for motivating examples of resilience. *Brave Women at Work* delivers. I was especially inspired by Kim Ellet's candid story of being at the intersection of Reinvention or Defeat and her seven wise steps to starting over. This book can be a catalyst for remarkable change for those who choose to read it, reflect on it and bravely take action."

—**Tricia Molloy**, Leadership Speaker and Author of "*Working with Wisdom*"

"*Brave Women at Work* - along with the brains behind it, Author and Coach Jen Pestikas - is warm and motivating! For anyone who needs an extra push or just to feel like there are others who have taken challenging paths and prevailed, this is a perfect read for you."

—**P. Fierst-Walsh**, Vice President, Traceability

DEDICATION

We dedicate this work to our daughters. May they find their brave and confident place in the world. And to our partners John and Brad, who are committed to the strength and success of those same young ladies.

Jennifer and Hope

Table of Contents

Prologue 1
Introduction to Shelia Higgs Burkhalter 5
   First, Only, Different (FOD) 7
Introduction to Kim Ellet 31
   Reinvention or Defeat 33
Introduction to Betsy Gornet 49
   What did I read? 51
Introduction to Georgie Komeiner 81
   Standing Tall 83
Introduction to Yalonda Brown 105
   Staying Power: Thriving in the Storm 107
Introduction to Trisha Tayan 123
   Wolf Bites 125
Introduction to Hope Mueller 147
   Only Speak When Spoken To 149
Introduction to Jennifer Pestikas 165
   On Fire, Back From Burnout 167
Epilogue 185
Discussion Guide 187
Acknowledgements 193

PROLOGUE
Jennifer Pestikas

> *"Resilience is knowing that you are the only one that has the power and the responsibility to pick yourself up."*
> —**Mary Holloway**

Each of us will be tested. Whether that's through illness, divorce, being told we're not enough, or career challenges, we have a choice. We can either rise to the occasion or resign ourselves to defeat.

In 2020, during the Coronavirus (COVID-19) pandemic, the global community was wrestling with moment-to-moment unknowns. We quarantined in our homes, unsure of what the next day would bring. I felt the pull of not wanting to watch the news, at war with the need to find a modicum of certainty in my world.

During one period of quarantine, I reflected on resilience and had an intuitive nudge to share women's stories. I wanted to give back during a period of such uncertainty. It was a way to thumb my nose at what was happening and reclaim a measure of control. An act of rebellion. An act of resilience.

At the same time, I was building my podcast, Brave Women at Work. I was fortunate to have Hope Mueller, pharmaceutical executive, speaker, and writer, on as a guest. We hit it off immediately. On a whim, I shared my idea of writing a book with her. Unbeknownst to me, Hope recently launched a publishing company, Hunter Street Press. Before I knew it, Hope and I reconnected, and she told me, "Let's do this!" With naive joy and a burning desire to help women, the *Brave Women at Work: Stories of Resilience* book was born.

As we've woven these chapters together, I have found comfort in the fact that struggle and the rising act of resilience are part of the human condition. Women often face more challenges than men, especially in career settings. In a 2021 study by Yale University, Professor Kelly Shue and her co-authors found that women got higher performance ratings than men but were consistently – and incorrectly – judged as having less leadership potential.[1] As women, we know that

---

[1] Managers Aren't Promoted Because Managers Underestimate Their Potential, Kelly Shue et al, Yale Insights

we are capable of leading, whether that's in the boardroom or at home. What this book provides is proof that women are resilient, inspirational, and powerful leaders.

My hope is that by reading this, you will be reminded that you are resilient and capable. That you can tackle the obstacles in your path. It doesn't matter the challenge; resilience is the act of getting up after being knocked down.

My closest family and friends know that my favorite movie is Rocky. New friends and colleagues are often surprised by this. Why Rocky? If you've never seen the movie, Rocky is an underdog and is expected to lose. He's mocked and discounted. It's through his hard work, grit, and determination that he rises to the top and wins the boxing champion title.

Women can be considered the "Rocky's" of today. We are often the underdogs and expected to lose, whether that's jobs, relationships, or opportunities. We are often silenced and discounted. It's through our hard work, grit, and determination that we will take our rightful place at work, home, and in society. When women rise, the world is a better place.

"Let me tell you something you already know. The world ain't all sunshine and rainbows. It's a very mean and nasty place, and I don't care how tough you are, it will beat you to your knees and keep you there permanently if you let it. You, me, or nobody is gonna hit as hard as life. But it ain't about how hard ya hit. It's about how hard you can get hit and keep moving forward. How much you can take and keep moving forward. That's how winning is done!"

—**Sylvester Stallone, <u>Rocky Balboa</u>**

INTRODUCTION TO SHELIA HIGGS BURKHALTER

For the past twenty-eight years, Shelia Higgs Burkhalter has worked in higher education. Shelia is a motivated and focused educator who is committed to student success and cultivating innovative, transformative, inclusive, and vibrant campus communities where excellence is expected, and collaboration embraced. Students affectionately refer to her as Shiggs.

Shelia is an accomplished speaker, facilitator, and a certified Executive & Leadership Transitions Coach. She specializes in helping aspiring executives and leaders to successfully transition to their next level of leadership. She believes in *people, values,* and leading with *heart.* As the owner of ShiggsB Coaching, she incorporates her knowledge of leadership, people, communication, and energy to create a transformational experience for her clients.

Shelia has a Managerial MBA from University of Arkansas - Fayetteville, an MSEd in Student Affairs Administration from Indiana University - Bloomington, and a BS in Mass Communication/Political Science from Southeast Missouri State University.

FIRST, ONLY, DIFFERENT (FOD)

Shelia Higgs Burkhalter

I transitioned into new positions, at new institutions, in new cities eight times now. I have done it as an unpartnered single woman, a partnered single woman, a married woman, and with a family in tow. Heck, I have even been a contributing author for a book about how to effectively plan and execute a job search and how to manage the transition. As you might imagine, I am skilled at spotting red flags, hearing what is not being said, noticing underlying messages, and parsing out the backstory when completing the environmental scanning of a new employment opportunity. Sounds intense? Well, it is. Making career moves involves my husband of twenty-two years who is a professional, and a teenaged daughter who has opinions about, well, everything. This journey is not just about making a living; it is about making a life.

I have learned that looking through the rearview mirror focused on where you have been or what you're leaving behind creates a blind spot for seeing what is ahead. I strive to keep my eyes forward with clarity about what I want and need, including a list of my negotiables and non-negotiables. This was absolutely the case in my last job search, or so I thought.

I didn't deign to type a single letter on an application unless the university met some critical criteria. A focus on the student experience, student success, and a visible commitment to diversity, equity, and inclusion (DEI) would be the driving catalyst for a deeper exploration. Visible evidence that an institution was 'walking their talk' was necessary. Finally, the rewards of a vibrant city coupled with the benefits of suburban living, proximity to family, familiarity with the area, and a robust position profile were necessary.

My search led to the identification of what seemed like an ideal opportunity. The vice president for student affairs opportunity at Winthrop University in Rock Hill, South Carolina, had the right title, the right portfolio, and the right location. It ticked all the boxes of being the right institution. Check. Check. Check. I applied.

I'd had a series of challenging past work experiences that made me question if I had paid close enough attention or asked the right questions during the selection and interview process. I was hypervigilant about understanding what I required for my next opportunity. Then I conducted validity checks to be sure that I'd recognize it when I found it. I conducted deep environmental scanning by reading any material within arms or virtual reach. I talked with individuals in my network who had knowledge of the institution. I had an action-packed interview experience that included a phone interview, neutral site interview (AKA airport interview) with a committee of twelve people, the provost and president, and a two-and half-day campus experience that included interviews with 75+ individuals and groups. I did solo and guided tours of the campus and city and a realtor tour. I met with a group of thirty students from a wide array of backgrounds and experiences. I even had an off-schedule conversation with a group of Black professionals at various levels of the institution to understand their lived experiences. I developed a three-page single spaced list of questions and unabashedly asked them all. I wanted to know precisely what I might be walking into if I was offered and accepted this position.

The answers to my questions weren't perfect, but they were open and honest. There were clearly challenges ahead, but there was nothing I didn't feel prepared to handle. After all,

I was a twenty-four-year seasoned professional transitioning from an eight-year chief student affairs role. I understood the sometimes-harsh realities of running a comprehensive institution. I knew the jargon and the hidden meaning behind certain phrases. I knew that a historic campus meant deferred maintenance. I knew that right sizing the institution meant budget reductions. I knew that realigning staffing meant permanent elimination of positions. The pros outweighed the cons; the highly relational Southern hospitality and the inclusive, innovative, engaging, and thoughtful interview process drew me in more deeply. The robust offer, the match with my non-negotiable list, the wonderful students, and the spirit of the colleagues with whom I'd be working sealed the deal. I said "yes" to the opportunity.

In hindsight, the deep significance and groundbreaking nature of my placement was all around me. Giant signs that I looked past. The offer of the 'off schedule' session with other Black professionals was a career first. I interpreted that as a cutting-edge DEI practice indicating to me that members of the committee recognized that my lived experience as a resident in the city and state might be starkly different from theirs. The after-dinner conversation where a future white male colleague asked how I anticipated handling being the only Black female at a leadership table that includes five white men was a bit disarming. Because my diversity definition is broader than the color of one's skin, the presence of three women and a Latinx man on the leadership team also represented visible diverse perspectives. I diplomatically, firmly shared that this was not my first experience being a first, only, different (FOD) – a term coined by the formidable Shonda Rhimes in her book, *Year of Yes: How to Dance It Out, Stand In the Sun and Be Your Own Person*, so the lack of people of color seemed routine in my experience, and something for which I was prepared. I explained with specificity how I had and would continue to navigate that world. The mere utterance of the question should have given me more clarity about the journey ahead.

In a group interview, I was asked how I would address potential DEI concerns with offending senior level colleagues. The position for which I had applied was not the chief diversity officer, so this question was vexing. Were these questions asked of other candidates? All candidates? In the moment, I answered the question with grace, directness, and surety. If offered the position, I knew that I would need to clarify expectations, choose which battles to engage and which to leave behind. These questions weren't intended to be mean or cruel; there seemed to be a genuine curiosity. There was a slight signal that my presence might disrupt or challenge the status quo, behavioral norms, and expectations at the institution. There was sincere interest in how I would handle challenges and the degree to which they'd have to endure discomfort in the process. There also seemed to be a regard for my feelings of safety, happiness, comfort, and success.

Being a FOD—a first, only, different wasn't new territory. These monikers had been my faithful companions as I entered spaces and places not designed with me in mind. It was my normal. While I saw, heard, and felt the whispers around me as I interviewed, they did not cause trepidation.

There was, however, a significance of my hiring that I did not see. It wouldn't be fully revealed until months after I joined the team. When I met Kevin, the Black custodian who prepared my office for my arrival, he told me he had shown up for my interview and knew that I was the one. He said he prayed over my office and for my resilience and success because "We need you." At that point, the significance of my hiring was a faint whisper.

I received a letter from the University Advancement indicating that someone had given a gift in my name to the Roddey, Johnson, Gladden, Meriwether Endowed

Scholarship fund, a fund that was dedicated to the first four Black women pioneers who integrated Winthrop in the 1960's. I was humbled at the thought that I was of the same ilk as these trailblazers. The donation, in my name, caused the whisper to become a mild buzz and was accompanied by a blinking light. The significance of my placement and role was blocked by the busy-ness of new beginnings: papers to sign, people to meet, problems to solve.

Then came my first Black Faculty and Staff meeting. I entered an old red brick academic building with wide hallways and photos from a bygone era. Thankful to be out of the heat of an early-September day, I made my way down the hall to the multi-purpose room. I entered the room with curiosity which blossomed into joy at being surrounded by the energy and spirit of welcome that comes from being with people who look like you and with whom you share similar experiences. After the meeting and greeting which included hugs, handshakes, and well wishes, we settled in for a discussion. A commanding faculty member, Clarence, one of the first Black faculty members in the College of Business, opened the meeting. He included in the introduction how long he and others had fought and positioned for more diversity within the upper echelons of the institution. He welcomed me and crystallized the significance of my presence and my role. I was a dream realized as the first Black senior leader in the institution's one hundred and thirty-two-year history.

The puzzle piece clicked into place. The picture was complete. The whirr became a siren. The blinking light became rotating, blaring alarm with strobe lights. The significance of my existence, in this place, at this time, and the weight of the responsibility crashed onto my shoulders. I was the living, walking, talking embodiment of someone else's dreams. Not unfamiliar territory. Different because this was not a family member or a personal dream. The oft times illusive, faceless 'they' were still here to see their dream realized. To them, I was *the* dream in the flesh. And they had their own ideas about how I came to be in the space and how I should occupy it. They had expectations for how I would represent them. The reality of the spoken and unspoken expectations took up space in my head, hovered over my shoulder, sat beside me in the boardroom, whispered in my ear, and occupied my thoughts.

There were other factors outside of the institution which added to the pressure I felt as the First Black woman in a senior leadership role in the institution's one hundred and thirty-two-year history. I arrived on campus a year and half after the Trump administration took office. The news headlines were full of reports about the audacious and catabolic leadership emanating from the White House. The presidency was often the topic of conversation, and there wasn't any political middle ground on that topic when discussed in South Carolina. Newsrooms and social media outlets were inundated with stories and images of the persistent and violent slaying of black and brown bodies. The Black Lives Matter Movement experienced a resurgence as the exhaustion, fear, and anxiety around the racial issues of the country reached a boiling point. Then the devastating, life-snatching COVID-19 pandemic arrived on the scene, taking lives in record numbers. It hit Black and Latinx communities at disproportionately higher rates, further raising the tension and stress surrounding the pandemic to an ominous level. It hit close to home when my family experienced the first two of what would become a wave of twelve deaths to COVID.

Meanwhile, on campus, I was head of a multi-pronged university division, with a multimillion-dollar portfolio, steeped in risk. My division was responsible for management of the torrent of day-to-day issues of running a campus outside of academics. My portfolio consisted of the police, counseling, health services, victim's assistance, disability services, the residence halls, campus center, recreation center/recreational services, conduct, behavioral intervention, care team, emergency funding, orientation, family programs, student diversity and special populations, student engagement, fraternity and sorority life, career services, civic engagement, food service, and the bookstore.

Exactly six weeks into my tenure, I was told by my supervisor, the provost, that she would be retiring at the close of the year. Two days later, the university president asked me to lead the search to fill the impending vacancy. It is assumed and expected that the answer to such an 'ask' will be 'yes'. I met 'the ask' with a series of questions to be sure I understood the scope of the assignment. Would a search firm be engaged? Would I have a co-chair? What support would exist for managing the search? How would the search team be selected? I was praised for the questions and got immediate answers.

I was excited that the president respected my search expertise and trusted me to lead this high-profile search for the next executive vice president and provost. I was deeply concerned about my ability to deliver on the expectations of myriad stakeholders—trustees, deans, faculty, staff, and students--who would provide input into, monitor, and scrutinize every aspect of the process. I was worried about how I'd meet the deliverables of my primary role as vice president for student affairs while ensuring that the search progressed. I didn't yet fully have my footing, and the world as I knew it felt like barely contained chaos. Still, I said yes because no didn't feel like an option. I leaned upon my knowledge and experience, tried and true processes from previous searches, my ability to quickly build rapport, willingness to ask questions and seek help, and to deploy support from colleagues to manage the process. I was purposefully swimming, but swimming.

I was also the chair of the Critical Incident Management Team (CIMT). In my first year, we dealt with issues like a major roof fire, a city water main break which shut down the campus, a high-profile sexual assault, a very messy, media involved Homecoming tailgate experience, and a student death. As I rounded the corner into the second year, I found myself facing an unexpected and contentious campus presidential transition which led to student activism with the Board of Trustees as the target. When your title is vice president for student affairs, the expectations of student management and control fall squarely within your responsibilities. In the world of students and student activism, control is an illusion. During this time, COVID-19 made its arrival on campus, and CIMT under my guidance was at the forefront of shepherding the campus through the dicey, ambiguous territory. The sea that I was swimming got very choppy. I developed occasional hives from the constant stress and the steady stream of cortisol and adrenaline flooding my body. My well-controlled hyperthyroidism flared causing sleeplessness, fatigue, weight loss, heart palpitations, and the jitters. Still, I swam.

The challenges inherent in my role were enough to keep me constantly almost overwhelmed. When you are first, only, different, it is a foregone conclusion that there will be a weightiness that accompanies you. It comes with the territory. This new knowledge of the significance of my arrival impacted me. Who I was, how I embodied my role, how I represented myself and others, what I said and didn't say became more meaningful than I had anticipated. My new role was not only laden with the avalanche of tasks inherent in managing a student body during political turmoil and a pandemic, but also the heavy yoke of expectation. Each word, each action I took might disappoint or please my supporters or hinder future opportunities for others who will undoubtedly come after me. There seemed to be both a conscious and unconscious, constant monitoring of everything that I said and did, and how I presented myself by others, and by myself.

The pressure of leading in this season was formidable. I was in real danger of losing sight of myself. I was in crises up to the crown of my head and barely able to come up for air. I found myself controlling what I could so that I could utilize my limited creative and innovative bandwidth to address the issues coming my way. I suppressed my initial reactions of worry, anger, frustration, and judgement for a responsive approach that considered the many perspectives before responding or acting. This approach allowed me to retain a spirit of service to my seat at the table and to the stakeholders that I represented. I was managing the weight of the load with a grace and boldness that comes from experience, knowledge, and self-assurance. It did not make the load less heavy. I restrained my stress and fear. I traded sleep for productivity. I worked fifteen-hour days, five days per week and sixteen hours more on the weekends. I used my communication and diplomacy skills to stay engaged and to buy time. I needed time to think, research, consult, and make well-considered, wise decisions. I was exhausted. I was treading water. I was getting it done.

During the all-consuming, high profile leading that I was doing, the realities of life as a Black woman in this country, in the state of South Carolina, and on my campus were taking a toll. I was stressed, tired, and wondered what the point was. There was a part of me that wanted to break free and shout my truth to anyone who would listen. This first, only, different Black VP was expected to possess a strong public persona, excellent communication skills, a high emotional quotient, and executive presence. Shouting in public was not a desired quality. Instead, I whispered my discontent in my prayers and asked God for strength. I buzzed about my stress in group texts with my sisters and best friend. I agitatedly relayed incredulous stories to my dad and mentors via the phone. At home, I shouted my discontent to my husband. It wasn't enough. I was tethered. I leaned into my spirituality through online church attendance, listened to self-help books while I walked my neighborhood, enjoyed uplifting music, watched inspiring movies, journaled, meditated per the recommendation from my doctor, and fell asleep to ocean sounds. That provided a measure of relief. I was still bound.

My husband encouraged me to pursue the coaching certification that I had endlessly researched and discussed but never initiated. He insisted I needed to do something just for me. I insisted the timing was all wrong. Adding more to my plate seemed ludicrous. Then the world pivoted to new ways of being. We all went home. The coaching program went virtual. There was no need to travel, no hotels, no coordination of school pick up and drop off. No rushing back to campus for evening and weekend events. I needed to back away from the fifteen-hour workdays, and I now could, periodically. Universities value education and support it. This coaching program would give me a legitimate reason to take regular breaks, and its purpose or legitimacy wouldn't be questioned.

The program was an unanticipated gift and lifeline. It included individual and group coaching. This new group of non-judgmental, detached but involved colleagues helped me to navigate my realities. The coaching program required me to regularly reflect in written form, which was cathartic. I identified my values and explored my thoughts, beliefs, feelings, and experiences. I deeply ruminated on my *what* and *why*. The program couldn't have come at a better time. I was reminded of the importance of values alignment and authentic living. These truths reasserted my foundation.

The triggering events of the loss of Ahmaud Arbery, Breonna Taylor, George Floyd, and Tony McDade brought back the urge to speak and act. Spurred by my values of responsibility, justice, and care, I reflected upon what I had done during my tenure at the University of Baltimore when Freddie Grey died. While diversity, equity, inclusion, and justice weren't my primary function, taking care of my students certainly was—then and now. Borrowing from that example, I commissioned the director of counseling and the assistant dean of diversity and student engagement to conceptualize support opportunities and outlets for processing for our students.

In our standing meeting, the executive vice president/provost and I discussed that the hurt, pain, and need for care wasn't confined to our students. She inquired whether we could do something as an institution. Institutional decisions impacting faculty and staff were not my call to make. I'd have to involve the new interim president. It was risky because what if this new president, about whom I knew little, wasn't supportive? His first introduction to me was through the unrest between the student government and the Board of Trustees. Had he already labeled me a troublemaker?

However, I was in a different space. I was no longer willing to be anchored to what I thought I was allowed to say and do. I approached the president and boldly shared my thoughts and ideas. He readily agreed with my suggestions, and I was encouraged to expand the charge to my two directors to include the campus Diversity Council, a committee consisting of faculty, staff, and students who are charged with helping actualize Winthrop's diversity goals and objectives as stated in the Winthrop Plan. After a series of meetings, the

Diversity Council suggested a community-wide conversation on racism.

The June 7, 2020, Diversity Dialogue: A Conversation on Racism Town Hall was billed as "an opportunity for faculty, staff, and students to have a platform to share and engage on issues related to race and social injustices." The goal was to "share your thoughts on how the community can move forward to become better change agents." In a season of utter hopelessness, I had leaned in and catalyzed an institutional response. My work was done. I could breathe again.

Then, I was asked to speak.

No instructions or parameters were given about how I should approach my remarks. I was the vice president who had gotten the ball rolling on this event. I was the first Black senior leader on the campus in 132 years. I was a Black woman with a Black husband and Black child living in America. The assumption was that I needed no direction or guidance. I could decide what I needed to say. I was both nervous and excited. A bit of the weight returned.

There was a variety of ways I could meet this moment. I struggled over how to approach the opportunity. I knew there would be trustees, faculty, staff, and students present. Community and political members might also be there. Because COVID was in full effect, the forum would be virtual and recorded for those who wanted to access it later. I knew that my comments might be misconstrued, or I might be misjudged. If my commentary was too abrupt or emotional, a loss of position could be the outcome which not only impacts me, but multitudes of others now and in the future. If I was too politically correct, tempered, or academic in my approach, my voice and my thoughts would not be heard and others would not be served. I had two minutes to make an impression.

I wrote my remarks in advance of the event and then practiced. They were informative, at points compelling, but still relatively safe. A whisper of discontent gnawed at me. I could do better.

I sat down and rewrote my remarks a day before the event. I included a story about how racism intersects the worlds of our students to anchor the urgency of addressing the issues. It was better, but the buzzing was back. Was this what I—from a leadership perspective and with my intersections of identity—needed to be saying in this moment?

The morning of the event, as I dressed myself for the day, the buzz was a siren. The giant blinking light was back. As I reflected upon the value of my seat at the table and the mantle that I was given, I knew that the Town Hall was the time to walk boldly into my freedom. I needed to give voice to my experiences and by association that of others. I had a seat at the table. Now was the time to embrace my values of justice, courage, and authenticity to utter the truths that would show the fullness of my humanity, not the caricature of humanity with prettied narratives that people carry about Black people who achieve greatness. I needed to share my personal story. I had two minutes.

I abandoned dressing for a few minutes, sat down on my chaise lounge, and let my fingers fly over the keyboard as the words poured out. Later that afternoon, as the Town Hall commenced, I was a bundle of nerves. Not because I was afraid to speak, but because I knew that my comments were going to be a surprise to the audience. I was going to be vulnerable in a way I had not done before with these colleagues and students. As my name was called, I steadied myself, looked directly into the camera, greeted the crowd, took a deep breath, and started to speak.

"As a professional, Black woman, I always have to think carefully about how to enter into conversations and spaces about polarizing issues. You see, there is always a possibility that I will say or do something that will make others feel uncomfortable, cause others to view me differently, ruin opportunities for others who look like me, or get me labeled. But I also find that when I am too careful, I continue to be burdened by the weight of my

lived experiences, and I do not use my power and privilege to illuminate the pain of others. I also miss out on the opportunity to educate and support people within my sphere of influence. So today, authenticity wins because hearing my stories as a vice president for student affairs gives the impact of racism a face.

In 1938, at the age of 10, my now 92-year-old grandmother and her family left Arkansas under the cover of darkness with bullets whizzing past their heads, because the sharecropper they worked for said that he'd see them dead before he'd see them leave that farm.

My 67-year-old father was raised in the segregated South where he was referred to as "boy" even after he had become a man. He drank from Coloreds Only water fountains, picked cotton, and when he went to school, he was not educated, because others decided he wasn't worth the investment. He's now a pastor who is regularly pulled over because he drives a nice car and wears a nice suit. That is reason enough for him to be suspicious.

At 19 years old, I interviewed for a receptionist job by phone and was hired instantly. This job was close to my college campus and would be my first opportunity to work from a desk rather than a fast-food counter. As I approached the front desk on my first day of work, I was greeted with a chilly stare of confusion and a "Can I help you?"

I introduced myself and indicated that I was there to fill out my employment paperwork. I was told, "You can't be Shelia Higgs. You're Black." When I produced my ID to verify my identity, I was told the job was no longer available.

At 48 years old, I still walk into rooms where I am a FOD—First, Only, Different—where I've learned to compartmentalize and temper my style, the strength of voice, and my approach in order to be accepted… to be non-threatening.

I am married to an educated Black man who won't step outside of our yard without proper identification, a cell phone, and keys…even when he is walking the dog 30 feet away from our front door, across the street in the park. I worry every time he goes out alone—particularly after dark. If he is even a few minutes late, I am texting or calling for an update.

We are raising a talented, intelligent, beautiful daughter whom we are empowering to walk into her greatness. Yet we are simultaneously preparing her for the moment when the color of her skin might be all that others see.

While many of my family members, friends, colleagues, and allies have developed tools that allow us "to keep on keeping on" despite the constant onslaught of traumatizing experiences and images. I worry about our students—all of you. I believe you need and deserve our support in navigating and changing this world.

You deserve to be seen and heard. And, you need to know that we are making a commitment to doing what we can, where we are, with what we have. Today's conversation about race is a start."

In the two minutes that I had, I chose to bring my whole, fearless self to the conversation. With integrity and unflinching, unapologetic honesty, and at times, a slight tremor in my voice, I shared my family's history and my lived experiences and story in a public, recorded forum of 400+ people. The question-and-answer period allowed me to challenge the status quo, advocate for change, and encourage others to do their own work. In that moment, I was both powerful and vulnerable. I did it for the audience because I wanted them to know that education, a high-powered job, a house in the right neighborhood, pretty suits, and success aren't enough armor to shield anyone from racism. I did it for me too. For the first time in two years, I was whole and free.

That moment was a defining moment in a sea of moments and choices; and since that day, I embody this role, this life, and live untethered. I am not reckless and am always well-considered. I acknowledge those who paved the way for me learning from their wisdom and their historical perspective. I have re-learned to trust my intuition. I make the choices that are authentic to who I am, without losing sight of whom I serve. I live free and have released myself from the weight of others' expectations.

This is your one life, your one opportunity to choose courage, authenticity, freedom, and joy. Choose well.

INTRODUCTION TO KIM ELLET

Kim's success is based on learning how to reinvent herself and releasing the kicking and screaming that often goes with it!

Some of her reinventions include going from a University of Georgia graduate to a career woman with numerous positions in the Hospitality and Meetings Industry, to full-time-parent, statewide community advocate as a Board Member for Georgia Parent Teacher Association (PTA), co-owner in multiple businesses, and then single mom, and back to school again.

Currently as a Leadership Coach, Diversity, Equity, & Inclusion Facilitator, and business owner, Kim helps leaders and teams get out of their own way to reach their big goals. She is passionate about collaboration and brings people together for crucial conversations and building bridges. Kim specializes in leadership coaching and development while assisting leaders with employee and board engagement.

Kim is a Certified Professional Coach and earned her credentials through the Institute for Professional Excellence in Coaching. She holds the Certificate in Diversity & Inclusion from Cornell University and is certified in Cultural Mastery. Kim is a graduate of the University of Georgia and began her coaching business in 2012. She has owned the Atlanta office of The Growth Coach since 2014.

You can read her Building Bridges newsletter on Linked In or reach out to subscribe. https://www.linkedin.com/newsletters/building-bridges-6922597370350223360/

Contact Kim for networking, executive coaching, and to learn more about building effective team communication. You can reach Kim on Linked In https://www.linkedin.com/in/kimellet/ or www.kimellet.com

REINVENTION OR DEFEAT
Kim Ellet

Years ago, there was a group called F.E.M.A.L.E., which was an acronym for Formerly-Employed-Mothers-At-Loose-Ends. I joined when my older daughter was months old and stayed until my twins were on the way two months later. The women I met in F.E.M.A.L.E. were in similar situations – trying to figure out who we were now that we'd traded our business suits for sweatpants and burp cloths. My loose ends weren't simply about motherhood and my soon-to-be three babies in eighteen-months reality. The loose ends began with my first reinvention – leaving behind my career-woman identity at thirty-six, to being a full-time parent. My former colleagues were shocked when they learned of this new phase of my life. I too was confused and dismayed. Up until then, I had defined myself by my business card. Who was I now, that I didn't represent a company or have a prestigious title? This was a real struggle especially during the months between leaving my employer and the arrival of my first-born. My fear, bewilderment, and consternation did not evaporate; it festered unresolved while I masked my doubt about who I was and what I was doing. Until then, my worth, my value was defined by what I accomplished at work, my title, how much money I earned. I hadn't put much merit in the stay-at-home parent identity. I was lost.

These re-defining or 'losing oneself' moments commonly stem from the occurrence of a significant event such as a diagnosis, losing a relationship or a loved one, a substantial business loss or change, a global pandemic, or an economic shake-up. An event where nothing is as it once was. I have experienced losing myself and my life's function more than once. It is not enjoyable and usually isn't easy to resolve when thrust out of our comfort zone. In these moments, it is important to realize one is at an intersection of: Reinvention or Defeat. Even then, the choice is not always clear. Some days, reinvention feels terrific, and other times, feelings of defeat beat the reinvention into submission.

What does it take to choose yourself rather than admitting defeat? The following steps may help you but are not linear – you won't finish one completely before going to the next.

This is a process, and all the steps are important – some need to be worked repeatedly. Grant yourself grace and keep at it. This is reinvention and winning rather than accepting and folding to defeat.

1. Stop Fooling Yourself

The first crucial step for a successful reinvention is to face the reality of the situation. What's not working? What is keeping you up at night? Or what are you ignoring that's not going away?

In 2009-2010, I tried to explain away or look on the bright side of what was happening in my co-partnered business. This was in the middle of the mortgage crisis economic downturn. I was a part-owner in a commercial general contracting firm then, and we had taken on a client that was out of our regular expertise. My partners outvoted me on my intuition that the client couldn't be trusted and that we should pass on this opportunity.

When the client filed bankruptcy after our work was completed, our small company was left holding the bag to pay all the subcontractors and vendors we'd brought on – and yet had not been paid ourselves. This was a turning point; we could lose the business. It was time to face reality. To understand where we were as a company, of course, but the more important reality I had to see was coming into focus. I stepped back, reflected, and saw the warning signs, to question the viability of the partnership, and how my own values did (or did not, as was the case) align with the other two shareholders.

I rationalized everything and succumbed into blind trust that everything was going to work out. It was true that things eventually did work out. Through perseverance and litigation, two years in court, there was a settlement with the bankrupt developer's reorganization process that allowed us to recoup the financial losses.

Then I had to take off the blinders to see our business partnership and company's core values more clearly. On April Fool's Day, I discovered that one of my business partners, who was also my husband, was not who I thought he was. He was leading a double life – starring in a movie I didn't recognize, and I wasn't his only leading lady. His lifestyle and business choices showed me that we were oceans apart from each other. I had to dissolve our business interests and divorce him, to save myself and my sanity. This was the harshest reality and the darkest of days I had ever faced. This is not a story about my former partner – or me being wronged. Sometimes it takes the most heart-breaking, unimaginable circumstances to crack us open; to be able to reinvent ourselves and put ourselves back together with intention. They say we are stronger at the broken places. This step of getting real with yourself is a prerequisite for reinvention – for creating and living a life that works on your own terms. Not only do you have to let yourself see it, but you also must let yourself feel it. All of it. There were days when I was so engulfed in my feelings that fluctuated from deep-rooted grief, to shock, despair, anger, rage, and victimhood. One of Kelly Clarkson's songs was popular then and became my anthem: "*What doesn't kill you makes you stronger.*" I listened to that song on a loop and kept my minister's words nearby, "If you are going through hell, just don't pitch a tent!" This was part of the process that helped me a little bit each day to keep from drowning and from throwing in the towel. Reinvention or defeat. I would not, could not, did not accept defeat.

2. How do you want it to be?

Once you are clear on what you are no longer willing to tolerate, the next step is to design the life, the business, the relationships, and the health and well-being that you want to experience. While creating this vision, it's important to take stock of what has been missing that you no longer want to overlook and what else needs to be discarded. How do you want to feel in your life? Design a life that works better to meet your present circumstances or create a new vision and new circumstances.

If you are unhappy in your job, for example, take time to visualize the environment and the type of work that resonates within you. Don't get caught up in the 'how to'. Don't get distracted by the details. Set aside the specifics of your title and where you want to work and focus on what the workplace *feels like*. Consider big picture parameters: are you working inside or outside? Are you with many team members or a smaller organization? What's the nature of the work? How are you spending your time? What's the compensation level and culture for advancement? Decide what other parameters matter to you and **write them down**. Some people thrive from working alone and want an arrangement with autonomy. Others prefer the teamwork community with co-workers socializing outside of work. There are not any right or wrong answers, simply preferences to define and a vision to design.

Let yourself dream big and be sure to get the "Yeah, but's" out of the way! It's easy to get stuck with linear and logical thinking, like "*Yeah, but* I could never do that because I am too old, or too young, or I'd have to go back to school," or a myriad of thoughts to keep us playing small. Put that thinking aside and gain clarity about what you really want. The obstacles can be addressed later.

As your picture starts to emerge, you must **write it down**. Then you can review it and concentrate on it. Ruminate. You can make this a part of formal intention setting or a prayer. It's a tool for discernment. With this clarity, consider if you can create this vision in your current business. If not, then you have factors to weigh out different opportunities to consider, and decisions to be made. Remember to dream big.

I had *'yeah, buts'* clamoring around in my head as I weighed out options for reinvention after my divorce. I used a lot of paper and reflection time, research, and prayer during this design phase. When I defined some of the parameters I wanted, it gave me a launching pad to move forward from. I didn't have everything figured out all at once, but I had to make decisions to move forward with and create how this new chapter of my life was going to look. I decided to go back to school for coaching training and credentials to support women business owners growing their companies. I added additional coaching tools to my practice over the years to continue encouraging continuous improvement, growth, and reinvention. I still do this today, honing my skills and furthering my education, adding tools for collaboration, and helping organizations with inclusion, diversity, equity, and improving company culture.

3. Obstacles/What's in the way or keeping you stuck?

Now that you have painted a beautiful and inspiring picture of the life you want to live, the next step is to evaluate what is getting in the way. Ask yourself why you are not already living this amazing professional and personal life. What additional skills or credentials are needed? Are there conversations you've been avoiding at work or with your partner? Focus on what really matters rather than spinning your wheels *wishing* instead of *acting*. Usually, the obstacles are fear, limiting beliefs, or stories we have believed for far too long.

I had a client who wanted to win the lottery. I asked her to describe why she was so focused on winning a game of chance for her life's vision, and she explained that she had this deep desire to travel the world but didn't have the money it required. The only solution she could envision was to win the lottery. Once we clarified that what she *really* wanted was to travel the world, we could brainstorm on more actionable solutions such as working in a travel-related field, or teaching English to students abroad, or asking her current employer for an international assignment. This is the power of focusing on what matters and what you want.

Another trap is the blame game. It's often easier to blame people or outside circumstances for what isn't going our way. Look at what you *can* control, though. During the most horrible situations or challenges, the only thing we can control is what we say, think, or do. You probably can't change a devasting diagnosis or prevent your employer from closing the doors, but you can manage your outlook. You can control what you think, and say, and how you chost to spend your time. Remember that we are either reinventing ourselves or accepting defeat.

Now that you have admitted to yourself what is keeping you stuck and what you want, let's move on to the next step for reinvention.

4. How committed are you?

How badly do you want this change, or would you rather complain? Check the victim, poor-me attitude, and replace it with new ways of thinking and doing. That counterproductive thinking can become a habit, so commitment and persistence are imperative. Some business leaders who share their frustrations with me are not ready to do anything about it. They say they don't like what is happening but are not willing to make any changes. The comfort zone is stronger than the pain at that point.

I can relate. It took a lot for me to face what was going on in my marriage and business partnership and to make a change. I did not want my family broken or our world shaken up. Since that part was already underway, I had to commit to writing a different ending to the story I thought I was living. What I realized was that the only thing I could control was what I did now. This was a scary reality too: recognizing that though I had been a business partner in our businesses (we also owned four retail franchises), I had not earned an actual paycheck in over twelve years. I was terrified. There were things to consider as I weighed out options. I was the parent that got the kids off the school bus, drove carpool, helped with afterschool homework and activities, cooked dinner, etc., so how could I abandon them to take a job and punch a time clock? I assessed what I wanted to teach my kids about relationship values; what I wanted them to learn about facing tough times and perseverance. I also wanted to be there for them – I had committed to raising them rather than hiring others to do so. I accepted a part-time remote job and signed up for classes. I began to build back my professional network while I evaluated what was next.

The thing about comfort zones is that we feel safe there, until we don't. It takes grit for people to push through those walls, and commitment to winning at this is key. It isn't easy, which is why the next step is so important.

5. Ask for and Accept Support

A fascinating phenomenon in our culture is the badge of honor that comes from doing things all by ourselves and not asking for help. Sometimes it is intertwined with a sense of shame that there is something wrong with us or we are burdening others if we need support. One of the most important components of a successful reinvention is to let others in – to figure out what you need and to let others help. Allow yourself to lean on others for physical and emotional assistance. There is a myriad of professionals that are trained, skilled, and enthusiastic about serving. Consider grief counselors, career or business coaches, therapists, attorneys, dog walkers, babysitters, meal and grocery delivery, your minister or Rabbi, healers, physicians, and housecleaners to be some of the posse you assemble to create some room for what's next in your growth. Include trusted friends to support you on this committee, your personal Board of Directors you are creating. It's helpful to think about the specifics and ask for exactly what you need. When your friends and colleagues say, "Let me know how I can help" – take it to heart and give them an answer.

For any lingering reluctance about reaching out for assistance, think about how wonderful it feels when you can help someone. Often the person helping feels like they received a gift by being able to contribute. Embrace your support team, and they will embrace you back.

6. Practice

Reminder: these are not linear, one-and-done steps. Reinvention and winning vs. defeat and giving up is an ongoing process that requires consistency and practice. The lather-rinse-repeat approach is the key to staying on track and getting back on track. Be encouraged to incorporate some tools and exercises to take care of your entire mind, body, and spiritual well-being. Here are a few practices I have found helpful.

<u>Mindfulness</u>: Quiet your mind to allow yourself to mentally rest. Our minds like to analyze, theorize, scrutinize, and sometimes terrorize our peace. Take time for deep breathing – intentionally noticing the breaths. While you are concentrating on your breathing, you are taking a break from thinking about the staffing issues, back-ordered supplies, or the other stressors you've been facing. Sometimes simply noticing that you are holding your breath while going about your day's activities is an important first step. Take a breath!

Mindfulness is about being present in the here and now. One of my favorite mindfulness activities is the chocolate exercise by Elizabeth Scott, PhD[2]. The idea is to take time to slowly notice everything that is going on with all your senses while savoring a piece of chocolate.

<u>Yoga and regular movement</u>: Our bodies need a sense of mindfulness too. Yoga combines body movement with meditation to quiet the thoughts as well. You can join a yoga class for accountability and guidance if that is of interest to you. Setting up a space in your home with room to roll out a yoga mat or your meditation pillow can be beneficial too. I gifted myself with a one-inch padded yoga mat that I roll out in my living room or bedroom for stretching, yoga poses, and quiet time. I love listening to a 20–30-minute guided meditation on one of my meditation apps while I stretch and breathe, and I feel a marked difference in my body movement and my peace of mind.

<u>Gratitude and shifting our prayer</u>: Dr. Wayne Dyer and Oprah Winfrey helped bring the idea of fostering an Attitude of Gratitude into the mainstream several years ago, and it's a valuable practice. This shift from focusing on all that we lack or what we fear to *appreciating all that we have* sets us on an entirely different course. You can start with simple steps like expressing, "I am grateful for the food I have to eat, I am

---

[2] How to Enjoy a Chocolate Meditation, Elizabeth Scott, PhD, Reviewed by Megan Monahan, www.verywellmind.com

grateful that I have a home/ house/ dog that loves me…". Fill in the blank and keep the verbal recognition coming. It's powerful to make a practice of saying the gratitude out loud in a constant stream of what you are noticing around you. A friend of mine does this when she is driving to her job. She starts by feeling grateful that she has a job, a car, clothes to wear. She continues with all she is noticing as she drives, "I am grateful that blue truck just stopped at the traffic light, I am grateful for my windshield wipers in the rain, I am grateful that the cherry trees are blooming today, I am grateful for the team celebration we have scheduled for Friday…". What we focus on expands, so the more we notice what is going right, the better we can enjoy what is around us, and the more others will enjoy our company as well.

Keeping a Gratitude Journal is another practice to regularly write down and shift our perspective. Check out May McCarthy's, *The Path to Wealth* for her unique approach to a gratitude journaling routine.

7. Grant yourself Grace

It takes commitment to reinvent ourselves and embrace the next chapter in our lives. Granting yourself grace is an essential part of the process. I encourage you to do so simultaneously as you are working through the rest of the process. Give yourself a break. Show yourself some love and patience. Think about what you would be saying to your best friend if they were going through what you are. Would you be unkind or impatient? Would you insist she take care of herself? What would you say and how would you think about your friend? If you would send a card or buy them flowers, do that for yourself, too. If you would encourage your friend to get a massage or take the afternoon off to explore a nearby nature walk, then consider taking care of yourself that way too. It's time to think of yourself like an important friend.

Life is a series of opportunities for reinvention or defeat. Stay true to yourself and remember, we only have control over our thoughts, words, and actions – so choose wisely and choose reinvention. Choose love for yourself and those around you. I hope these steps and process bring you peace and remind you to live your life with boldness and joy! You've got this! We would love to hear from you with your stories of triumph and courage.

INTRODUCTION TO BETSY GORNET

Betsy leads The Sonnet Group where she consults, advises, and coaches leaders, clinicians, and teams to advance organizational goals, optimize performance, and resolve patterns of thinking and behaving that are barriers to achieving desired outcomes. Betsy brought her passion for improving the delivery of care for patients in need into working with a wide variety of healthcare organizations, executives, leaders, and their teams. Throughout her career, Betsy has observed the untapped potential within healthcare organizations for problem solving and innovating if not for the stress, overwhelm, disengagement, and lack of clarity people experienced day in and day out. These kinds of issues impacted not just individuals, but groups and teams charged with tackling critical issues facing their organizations. Yet, when those burdens eased, the possibility for sustainable improvement in patient care and strategic advancement were readily available.

Betsy holds an MS in Health Systems Management, is a Fellow in the American College of Healthcare Executives, and a credentialed professional coach and team coach. She is also a Transformation NLP Practitioner. Throughout her career, Betsy has been an active member of various professional organizations, served as faculty, a national speaker, and author on topics related to advanced illness management and end of life care.

WHAT DID I READ?

Betsy Gornet

In the 2012 movie, The Avengers, there is a scene where the Hulk, a large powerful green humanoid, falls from space through a warehouse ceiling and crash-lands on the floor, creating a small crater. As he transforms from the Hulk into the mild-mannered Dr. Bruce Banner, there's a security guard who witnesses the fall and asks the Hulk if he is an alien. Bruce says, "No." The security guard responds, "Well, then, son, you have a condition."

Fortunately, I don't have Dr. Bruce Banner's condition, but I do have one that I've struggled with my whole life – dyslexia. Dyslexia is more frequently heard of today than when I was growing up. Still, it remains a hidden disability. Somewhere between 5-20% of the population in the US experience some level of dyslexia.[3,4,5,6] Similar prevalence rates exist around the world regardless of language, age, ethnicity, or educational system. Even so, it is estimated that only a small percentage (5%) of those with dyslexia receive support and proper training for their condition. Sadly, often out of frustration and despair, students with dyslexia drop out of school at a rate of 35%, double the national average dropout rate.[7] Of those students who make it to college, it is estimated that only 34% are expected to graduate within eight years.[8] The International Dyslexia Association defines dyslexia as follows:

"Dyslexia is a specific learning disability that is neurobiological in origin. It is characterized by difficulties with accurate and/ or fluent word recognition and by poor spelling and decoding abilities. These difficulties typically result from a deficit in the

---

3   Shaywitz SE, Holahan JM, Kenney B, Shaywitz BA. The Yale Outcome Study: Outcomes for Graduates with and without Dyslexia. *J Pediatr Neuropsychol.* 2020; **6:**189–197 https://doi.org/10.1007/s40817-020-00094-3

4   Dowson, R. Dyslexia – the least known, most common learning disability." *The Alberta Teacher's Association Magazine;2084(201)* https://www.teachers.ab.ca/Publications/ATA%20Magazine/Volume%2084/Number%201/Articles/Pages/Dyslexia%20The%20Least%20Known%20Most%20Comm

5   Moats LC, Dakin KE, Basic facts about dyslexia & other reading problems. Baltimore, Maryland, International Dyslexia Association, ©2008

6   Hettiarachchi D. An overview of dyslexia. Sri Lanka Journal of Child Health. 2021; 5-(3):529-534 DOI: http://doi.org/10.4038/sljch.v50i3.9741

7   Addenbrooke S. Understanding the dyslexic drop-out: why students with learning disabilities graduate at a lower rate than their peers. Yale Education Studies. http://debsedstudies.org/dyslexic-drop-out/

8   National Longitudinal Transition Study-2, National Center for Special Education Research, "The Post-High School Outcomes of Young Adults with Disabilities up to 8 years after high school." 2011. Accessed: https://ies.ed.gov/ncser/pubs/20113005/pdf/20113005.pdf

phonological component of language that is often unexpected in relation to other cognitive abilities and the provision of effective classroom instruction. Secondary consequences may include problems in reading comprehension and reduced reading experience that can impede growth of vocabulary and background knowledge." [9]

Today, dyslexia is believed to result from a combination of factors. Having a family member with dyslexia increases the likelihood of having dyslexia. Brain-based differences specific to reading, vision, and hearing, as well as cognitive and perceptual differences are also factors. Environmental conditions or influences can also have an impact. Someone once told me, "If you have seen one dyslexic, then you've seen one dyslexic," referring to the wide variations seen between dyslexics, their symptomology, their coping strategies, and co-existing (co-morbid) conditions such as ADHD, depression, and anxiety. Dyslexia is referred to as a learning disorder specifically related to reading and language. For me, that cuts short of what's really going on. It impacts speech, writing, reading, comprehension, specific types of memory, math skills – and as a result, often impacts socio-emotional aspects of a person's life. It certainly has in mine.

---

9   International Dyslexia Foundation. IDA Fact Sheet, Definition of dyslexia. http://eida.org/definition-of-dyslexia/

My first realization that I was different came in first grade in Tulsa, Oklahoma. I sat with my classmates on the cool linoleum floor of a pre-fab classroom. There were fifteen of us eagerly listening to the teacher, Mrs. Lesson. She had written a sentence on the chalk board and asked if someone would read her the sentence aloud. Several students quickly raised their hands, and Mrs. Lesson called on a boy. The student read the sentence aloud. Mrs. Lesson smiled, apparently pleased. I let out a small gasp because that wasn't the sentence I saw on the board. I looked over at the boy to see if he was reading from a book. No, he was looking at the chalkboard. This is dyslexia: a lifetime of seeing, reading, hearing, and writing something differently than other people. The confusion and the frustration were new to me then but became commonplace in my life. When I was young it was an everyday struggle to match up the visual appearance of a letter, to name that letter, and identify the sound it makes – and the sound it makes when it is next to other letters. That decoding process can be excruciatingly difficult for dyslexics. And it feels like once you figure it out, you have only figured it out for that one time. Next time, it will look different or sound different, thus requiring you to figure it out-- again. Learning to read and decipher language feels slippery to someone with dyslexia. When you think you have it, it escapes like sand between your fingers - or in this case through the cracks in your memory. This is the experience of a person living with dyslexia, particularly one that has not benefited from the instructional support, development of compensating strategies, and use of assistive devices that are now more widely available.

Interestingly, reading a word on a page eventually got easier for me. If the font was of a certain type, the color of the paper was easy on the eyes, and there were no other graphics on the page. I began to discern words more discreetly and remember their meaning. However, if I was asked to sound out a word in elementary school, I might have been able to take wild guess. By the time I was in junior high, I could sound out letters better, but could not yet put them together to make a word. To me, the sound of a word and the sound of the individual letters never matched. It made no sense. This didn't happen every single time, but often enough. The real frustration was not having the language to describe what was going on for me. Often, my teachers and 'reading helpers' would just keep telling me to try again. To listen to how they do it and try again. The mechanics of what I experienced, though, were only the half of it. There was an emotional component to all this as well. I was petrified to read aloud. My voice would get shaky, my heart would race. I'd pretend to have a coughing fit if I thought it was going to be my turn to read aloud in class, or I'd try to distract the teacher by asking a question. I tried all kinds of maneuvers, even if only in my head, to figure out ways to not have to read aloud or to even answer a question about spelling, pronunciation, the meaning of a reading, and especially any question about grammar.

The bigger problem, though, as I got into higher level grades, was comprehension. Oddly, I felt confident about the content when I finished a reading assignment, only to find out that what I thought I gleaned from the reading was not at all what the reading was about or there were significant pieces of information I missed or misunderstood. Sometimes I got parts of it correct. Fortunately, I was driven and loved to learn, even when it seemed like learning didn't love me back. I was an eternal optimist, believing that next time, I would get it right.

In the 1960s-70s, dyslexia was barely a known condition by psychologists, let alone known by teachers. Sure, everyone at school knew I was a poor reader, and they did offer extra reading support from time to time, but it wasn't specific to my condition and mostly made both my teachers and me more frustrated. Also, at that time, no one appreciated the fact that standardized assessments were designed for the neurotypical student (neurotypical wasn't even a word back then). Consequently, in seventh grade, when the national education and intelligence assessments were completed I was invited to the guidance counselor's office to review my scores. Typically, this kind of meeting would occur with parents. However, my parents travelled often and were out of town. The counselor walked me through the assessments and told me that my teachers would be following up with me to offer more learning support. Bottom line, I was working well below grade level and my IQ score was well below average, closer to the developmentally disabled range. The counselor told me that school would get harder and harder for me with each new grade level. That going forward, schoolwork would be more demanding. The main takeaway from that conversation was simple: I may not make it through high school, and it would be unlikely I'd get into college, even if I were to graduate high school. I shut down when I got the gist of this message. My head filled with the sound of static, and I wanted to run from the room. It seemed so impossible that it was true. I didn't feel that different from my peers. I knew I struggled with reading, but there were other things I did well. The increasingly loud white noise in my head blocked his words. The counselor talked with me for a while, but I don't think I registered much of the information until days later. I walked back to my classroom with two competing thoughts swirling in my head. How could this be possible? I don't feel that incapable. I know things. The second thought, even more worrisome and beating in my head, was my life was over. If I can't go to college and maybe not even finish high school, what would happen to me then? I'm quite sure I didn't hear anything the rest of the day, even for a few days. I was assigned to the reading lab for one period every day and barely remember anything about it. For weeks, I fretted about my parents' reaction when they returned home. My deepest fear was that I would no longer be welcome in my family, that they might not love me, and would abandon me. I was the youngest of four and knew that reading well and attending college were highly valued expectations in my family.

My parents returned home a month later and it was never discussed. I don't know if the school ever talked with them. My parents never mentioned it to me, and I never asked. It would be another six years before we ever had a conversation about my challenges. I carried my deepest fears, choosing instead to focus on what I was asked to do at school and at home, to the best of my abilities. My parents did have me take different speed-reading courses outside of high school. None of which helped and were overall demoralizing for me. Nothing seemed to help, so I continued to try to get by each day without putting too much attention, or more accurately, trying not to draw too much attention, to my struggles.

Were it not for my love of athletics, specifically gymnastics and swimming, I would not have survived. In sports, there was a direct correlation between what my mind wanted or expected and what my body did. And when I didn't get the result I wanted, I could make a change and see 'for real' whether it worked. If I was on a balance beam, my mind and body worked beautifully together to keep my balance, recover from a wobble, and overcome the fear of learning a new skill. It was a reliable connection. Or if I were swimming too slowly, I knew how I could speed up and see the result right away. I felt an internal locus of control that linked my mind and body together. With this knowledge, I started to try to find that kind of place in my schoolwork. It was, and still is, a work in process.

Despite the outcome of my seventh-grade assessments, I made it through high school. It wasn't easy, and all the challenges my guidance counselor said I would face, I did. After taking the SAT's twice and applying to universities, I was accepted into college. Privately, as I began my first day of college at Indiana University, I hoped my struggles were behind me – that this was going to be a brand-new start. Well, that hopefulness was short lived, but relief was on the horizon.

Like a lot of first-year students at a large university, I took Psychology 101 my first semester in a large lecture hall filled with eighty or more curious freshman. I enjoyed the class and participated actively in discussions we had in class. When it came time for the first test, I did all the reading and prep work, just as the professor recommended to the class. I felt confident in my understanding of the material and well prepared for the first test. But I failed the test. Fortunately, my professor was curious about my test score and spoke with me about it. Initially, he referred me to the student center to be assessed for 'test anxiety'. When that didn't turn out to be the case, we had a follow up discussion and left it with – let's see how the next test goes. After I had taken the second test, with comparable results to the first test, he asked me details about how well I thought I knew the material. I was confident in what I knew, and I didn't understand why that wasn't visible on the test. Then he suggested we go through the test orally. He read each question and each multiple-choice option and I responded with my answer. He asked me questions about my confidence in my responses and why I had that confidence. He took notes as we went along. Turns out, by taking the test orally, I would have only missed two questions. Based on the difference between the written exam versus the oral exam, he referred me to the student learning center for a comprehensive learning disability assessment. I never would have been properly assessed for a learning disorder and identified as having dyslexia were it not for his curiosity and willingess to help me figure things out. It wasn't until years later I realized what a gift this professor gave me. I have forgotten his name now, but as part of this project, I researched the current professors in the School of Psychology in hopes that I may thank him. None of their names nor pictures looked like the professor I remembered. I can only hope, given his profession, he knows the difference he made in my life. I owe him my deepest gratitude.

While away at college, my parents had a rule about calling home every Sunday evening. I'll never forget the Sunday evening call when I shared my news about having dyslexia and how it explained my challenges. They couldn't make sense of it and thought for sure someone was steering me in the wrong direction. Fortunately, my sister, who held a Master's in Education and was a high school teacher, helped my parents match up my historical challenges with reading and what was known about dyslexia at the time. During the next Sunday evening conversation, I remember my mom saying, "We had no idea." Yes, that was true, and they weren't the only ones.

Even more important than the diagnosis itself, was the help I received following the diagnosis. I had the opportunity to participate in a program to learn compensating strategies for students with dyslexia. It was not a simple journey; it took three years for the compensating strategies to become more automatic. It took extra energy, focus, and practice, atop of an already full load of courses. I did cut back in the number of classes I took each semester and ended up in summer school most years. I finished college with a BA in Psychology and two minors – Mathematics and Computer Science. Additionally, I served as a research assistant in a psychopharmacology lab throughout college and was a co-author of the published research the year after I graduated. So, just to be clear - dyslexia doesn't mean you can't read or that you're not smart. It means how you go through the task of learning and how you get things done has to be different, which inevitably includes spending at least double the time and energy studying than most students.

As I graduated college, I had a plan. I was engaged to be married and I had a laboratory assistant job lined up. When I returned home from my honeymoon that job had fallen through. I ended up serving as a full-time substitute teacher for a high school. That was certainly something I never thought I would do. Turns out, I was the only registered college educated substitute teacher in Indiana at the time, which meant when a teacher went out on medical leave early in the school year, I was assigned to that role for the rest of the year. While I was teaching, I took the time to consider my career options. I wanted to pursue an advanced degree, preferably in the sciences or healthcare areas, but I was filled with doubts about my capacity to manage the work. Adding to my concerns were precautionary, albeit well meaning, warnings from family and friends that 1) graduate school would be an even higher level of difficulty and I might not make it, assuming I would get a high enough GRE score to get accepted to a graduate school; and 2) I should be careful about my career path towards anything where my having dyslexia may put others at risk should I switch words around or write down the wrong thing, or reverse right and left, etc. I found these kinds of comments incredulous. At the same time, I wondered if they could be true. Could I be a danger to others? Looking back, it's one of my greatest regrets: I let the fear of something bad happening at some time in the future deter me from following my initial passions and instincts. Back then, there were no role models to look to, no online mentors to ask questions to and get guidance from. There wasn't even much reading material on the topic that was written for the person living with the effects of dyslexia. For all I knew, these kinds of warnings needed to be taken seriously. It left me filled with swelling self-doubt and deep questioning around my ability to be useful, fulfill my purpose (whatever it may be) or contribute to society.

Remarkably, I went to graduate school, earning a Master of Science in Health Systems Management from Rush University in Chicago, Illinois. There were several factors that made graduate school less difficult than I had expected. First, all the courses ranging from sociology, to economics, to human resources, to law, all related to healthcare. That simplified the frames of references, the vocabulary I now had to learn, and reduced the variables. And importantly, I had years of training on how to compensate for my dyslexia. The second crucial factor, and the one that allowed me to complete my thesis, was the growth of personal computing. At that time, we could save our work on floppy disks and take it home and work on our home computer and then bring the disk back the next day to school and work on it some more. The third factor that helped me through graduate school was discovering one of my professors was also dyslexic. Finally, I had met someone, even one who was an accomplished scholar, of whom I could ask questions and learn from her experience. She struggled with numbers (she was a Statistics and Accounting professor), and I struggled with words. We had a side-bar agreement to help each other notice when something was mixed up or confusing.

I left graduate school with high grades, a completed thesis and internship, and two years of professional work experience under my belt. It helped me launch my career in a positive direction. I now had my degree, proven my ability to learn, and I could put all those worries about dyslexia behind me. I hadn't grasped yet that dyslexia was something you live with and struggle through in diverse ways your whole life.

At work, like school, things took longer. In school, I studied 3-4 times as long as the average student. In the 'real world,' it wasn't studying per se, it was doing work, reading material, drafting reports, preparing for meetings, creating presentations, analyzing data. I got it done, but it took me longer than it would others. I didn't see it as a big deal, though. To me, it was just necessary. I got up early and stayed up late to get the work done. Gratefully, I'm one of those folks who function well on four hours of sleep at night. And importantly, throughout my career, there were assistants who graciously proofed my writing and double-checked my work. Without them, I would not have survived or achieved as much success. Of course, the advent of desktop computing also helped. I was in graduate school before desktop computing became a reality. I'm certain that dyslexics across the world gave a collective cheer to have access to a life transforming tool such as word processing and spell check.

For most of my adult life, I've 'hidden' my dyslexia. The era of disclosing disabilities and accommodations is a new phenomenon in the workplace. When I entered the workforce, I didn't want to do anything that might give others the chance to discount my abilities. For my career, it felt as if disclosing my struggles would put credibility, reliability, trustworthiness, and promotability on the line. It would be lovely to report that things went smoothly once I entered the professional world. On the outside, it certainly looked that way. I was well positioned with a decent salary, and there was a clear career path ahead of me. However, there were times when all my efforts to manage the impact of dyslexia leaked out. Under unusually high periods of stress, my normally hidden disability became visible to others.

The first experience I had with this dyslexia 'leakage' problem was early in my career. I was an Associate Executive Director for a large tertiary hospital in Las Vegas, Nevada. Unexpectedly, I started noticing how hard it was to write the simplest of notes without making a bunch of errors. I noticed, too, that my typing was so inaccurate that I couldn't even tell what I meant to type and was having to start over as a result. I was also experiencing other signs of stress beyond those related to dyslexia. I started doing the most annoying thing – spilling my glass of water on my desk every day. It was so bad that someone brought in a package of paper towels and a sippy cup for me to keep on hand. One day, while helping me mop up yet another spill, an executive assistant whispered across the desk, "Something is going on with you. Perhaps you need to see someone, like a doctor or a therapist." I looked up at her and nodded.

The following week, I began seeing a therapist. Our sessions covered all the vital details going on in my life – my marriage and pending divorce, and my challenge with work-life balance. I never once thought to mention my dyslexia. I didn't think of it as something I was managing. It simply wasn't something I could let interfere with my life, or more specifically, my career.

The vulnerability of being in a position where others might notice my struggles with dyslexia was something I endeavored to avoid. I was afraid others would begin to question everything I said, or every analysis I did, or every decision I made. I didn't know if that would be true, but that's what it felt like to me. My biggest fear was losing credibility and the sense that I could be relied upon. I had to be able to get through stressful times without having my dyslexia 'leak out'. I had to figure it out, so I made a plan. Literally, I wrote myself a plan. It included a few key priority areas such as: 1) designating specific times to think about work vs. personal matters. I gave myself allowances for processing emotions, say five minutes, if they welled up inside me while I was at work. 2) Sleep time needed to be for sleep and not for thinking, or running through every 'what if' scenario my brain could conjure up. 3) I set boundaries for myself. I put a pad of paper next to my bed, and I would park any thoughts swirling in my mind onto that pad of paper so that I could work on it the next day. If I woke up in the middle of the night ruminating on some topic, I'd write it down and physically say to myself, "There, now it's parked for the night." Part of getting more sleep was also figuring out a way to take fewer 'on call' shifts afterhours and weekends. I was able to collaborate with other administrators on the team to distribute 'on call' time more evenly, and 4) I established an intention to slow down. This was the hardest task I assigned myself. I figured, if I continued to move at the speed I was moving, I'd continue to make mistakes and not catch them. I practiced settling into my chair, taking a breath, and then beginning what I needed to do. I noticed every time I tried to do something quickly, I'd forget something, write things wrong, misunderstand something, and it would end up costing me more time. Better to go slowly in the first place than doing it twice.

Slowing down was the best thing for me to do. This is a lesson I've had to repeat learning over the years. When I am intentional about giving myself time and space, it serves me well. It allows for more confident decision making, as well as more opportunity for innovative thinking to occur. Whenever possible, I consciously take time to make decisions even when I think I know the answer right away. I'll sleep on it. It has made an enormous difference in my success. These few ideas have been helpful for me not just in managing the effects of living with dyslexia, but also for managing stress and creating more of a work/life balance. This basic plan is a foundational piece for helping me cope and manage my daily life.

After initiating these changes, and of course, getting through the worst of my divorce, things evened out. Not immediately, but over time. Additionally, I hadn't realized how much my self-confidence had been eroded until it started to return. I was shaken by how visible my dyslexia had become at work. It left me vulnerable, and I had to be extra careful with my work and highly aware of input I received from others. It made me tentative – not something I normally experienced. During the times when I didn't trust myself – my brain and body – to do what I asked it to do, it was an awful place to live in. It was important for me to find my way back to that place where I felt a greater locus of control within myself, so that I could reference the skills and life stance I needed.

At the age of thirty, I became the CEO of a community organization that operated a specialty hospital, a home health agency, and a hospice. As the senior executive, every minute of the day I was aware that something might happen in the organization - to a patient or to a staff member – and that it was my responsibility. I was passionate about my organization's value to the patients and community we served. The organization, though, was on the financial brink of having to close its doors forever.

The pressure was immense. Fortunately, the passion I felt was greater, which kept my energy and focus fueled. Even with that, I could gauge my level of fatigue or stress by the visible signs of my dyslexia challenges – the 'leakage'. For example, if I looked at a flipchart I had just written and there were a lot of errors, I knew I wasn't getting enough rest. If I did an analysis and the Chief Financial Officer couldn't follow it, I knew I was under stress. If I gave a presentation and the audience suddenly looked like they were totally lost, I knew I was not feeling grounded enough to compensate for the dyslexia automatically. Fortunately, these kinds of days were rare. Looking back now, gauging my stress by how visible my dyslexia was, was like waiting until the road ends where the bridge gave out to make the decision to turn around. It's a little late.

The people I worked with every day thought I had a rock-solid memory and an eye for connecting the dots between patient care, processes, operations, and finance. They often told me that I had a knack for seeing important connections others miss – the inter-relatedness of unrelated data points. Those were accurate descriptors of my strengths, but it felt fragile to me, like it took constant maintenance of the pillars that supported me to make that possible. Those pillars were all the things I did every day to competently compensate for the dyslexia and frankly, manage the stress that builds up in both personal and professional aspects of life. I was confident I could make a difference and knew I had the skills, experience, and a talented team to help the organization turn around. I felt fortunate to have that awareness. To know my strengths and understand how to lean on other people's strengths too. It is important for people with dyslexia to discover their strengths and recognize their gifts.

There are hundreds, if not thousands, of examples of ways my dyslexia showed up in both my work and personal life as an adult. Sometimes it made me laugh, sometimes it made me cry. Mostly, though, it's been just part of my everyday life. I've had to settle into a continuous process of figuring it out. Partnered right alongside that figuring it out process was the willingness to begin again. At least until I couldn't.

In 2015, I was as working as an executive for a large regional health system leading an innovation project. I was working on a system-wide project supported in part by a multi-million-dollar governmental research award. We were in the final year of the research portion of this project, and it was a data intensive, report writing intensive, and presentation intensive period. There was a steady full stream of demands coming from both internal and external stakeholders. I had started with the project in its design phase back in 2009 and was now responsible for its operations and expansion across Northern California. As the project matured, I was spending increased time tackling the demands of the job. It wasn't uncommon that I would be in meetings, or on my computer, with barely a break, for ten to sixteen hours a day. And this had been going on for years. Then things started to fall apart for me. It started with simple things like – I couldn't remember writing an email. Or I didn't remember that I read something. One morning, I came to work only to find a report sitting on my desk. I figured someone else had put in on my desk. It turned out, I had drafted the report, but I couldn't remember. Then it was bigger things like the day I threw away my purse. Days later, I found it when I was taking out all the trash at home. Another time, I arrived at my favorite Pilates class, changed my clothes to go workout, and then in a blink of an eye, I thought I had finished class, and changed back into my street clothes. Had the instructor not stopped me as I approached the door to leave and asked what was going on, I would have driven home.

Worried that something was seriously wrong with my memory, I scheduled a visit with my primary care physician. Thankfully, I passed all the typical in-office memory tests with excellence. However, given the types of memory issues I was having, she referred me to a neuropsychologist for a comprehensive assessment.

As the assessment began, I was asked about my health history, mental health status, presence of any known disabilities, etc., I mentioned that in college I was identified as having dyslexia (through assessments). I almost didn't share that information. What if it wasn't true? What if I don't have dyslexia? I remember thinking to myself, even after all those years, I still found it hard to accept my diagnosis. Or perhaps, I was still having difficulty admitting to others that it existed? Interestingly, after the testing was completed, the neuropsychologist mentioned that in his thirty-year career he'd never had an adult client with dyslexia who also had a professional leadership career. People who are not having problems typically don't see him. After completing the day-long assessment process, he explained that I'd receive a written report in a couple of weeks. In the meantime, he offered to talk through the observations he gathered through the course of the day. He also included what compensating strategies he saw me use during the assessments. That was fascinating to me. There were things I do that I just took for granted, even thinking that everyone must do those things.

That day, I learned two important things. First, thankfully, I did not have any symptoms of a tumor or signs of early dementia. Phew! Secondly, he estimated that with the severity of dyslexia I showed in the testing, 25-30%, maybe more, of working memory was being used for compensating strategies alone. As a result, it was likely my brain was putting aside more mundane elements, like the location of my purse for example, so that it had enough working memory to complete the more complex tasks. Most importantly, though, I learned that this memory problem would continue for as long I continued to work in the ways I had been. The doctor recommended making modifications to the type and duration of work I did each day.

This information was a shock to me. I never considered my brain as having limits. Sounds funny to say that, but it's true. I believed there was always a possibility of making internal adjustments that would help me figure things out. I had outstanding endurance to use my brain. When others at work reported feeling 'tapped out' after a long meeting, I never felt fatigued. I was like the Energizer Bunny on the commercials on TV; I just kept going. I certainly never expected to have my brain hit a limit such that I might lose basic details like where my car was parked or the fact that I had drafted an email. Certainly, I needed to consider what changes I could make in the short-term to ease the memory burden. I also needed to consider what impact, if any, this had long-term for my career choices.

Right away, I started making changes. I identified other team members who could give presentations and empowered them to do so. I delegated to skilled staff members to work on graphics for PowerPoint presentations. I started taking power naps during lunch in my car - ten to fifteen minutes of rest made such a difference. I learned that taking breaks, even if only for a minute or two every hour or so, made a difference for me. I got up and moved around, looked out into the distance, relaxed, and breathed. Eventually, I also tried to teach myself to sleep longer than four to five hours each night. This was the hardest thing to change, and it has taken me years to do it. Fortunately, with these initial few changes, I saw improvements in my memory right away. This immediate improvement reassured me.

It was scary to think that my brain could decide on its own what was important to remember and what wasn't. That it could get full. How would I know if I'm reaching that threshold again? Could I predict it by the number of hours of work, or by the type of work? Or by how many hours of sleep I got each night? Or, simply by how easy it was to find my purse in the morning? All those types of parameters seemed outrageous. The complex set of compensating strategies I'd employed all these years have made it possible for me to have a career, to enjoy my passion around the work, and to have a sense of contributing in ways that matter. Was it too much for me?

I don't think so. Figuring out the balance of the type of work was important, exploring options was vital, and keeping a watchful eye on those internal cues that tell me I need a break also mattered. A year after the neuro-psych assessment, the culmination of the research project, and with the health of my son in question, I decided to step out of my role and look at how to reconfigure my life and profession in ways that better suited me. I took six months off to focus on my family and my own well-being. Then I went back to school to become an executive leadership coach and team coach. Now

I coach and provide advisory/consulting services to health care organizations, their leaders, and their teams.

There's more to dyslexia than it being a learning disorder. It's like a soccer player who has a strong right kick but a weak left kick. The player who wants to be successful practices and practices until each type of kick is equal to the other. That's what I've been doing every time I look at or read something. I look at something, triple check that it's in its proper order, that it makes sense and the meaning I'm taking from it is correct. I do that in my head – all day long. Over time, despite my timidity around sharing my challenges with dyslexia, I've developed assertiveness around asking for what I need. I now ask someone to remove the color background to an email and change the font to a standard format so that I can read their email. I've never had anyone refuse to make the changes I needed. When my kids were young I became more discerning about which books I would encourage them to enjoy alone and which ones I would read to them. Too much artistry or fancy writing styles made it impossible for me to read. Another area where I've developed workarounds is at a restaurant that has a menu designed in such a fashion that I can't read it. I've learned how to ask questions of the server to figure out what I would like to order or ask the people with me to read it to me or recommend something.

It isn't simply about learning; it's about how the world, my internal world, and the external world, sync up - each day. Appreciating that fact suggests further research is needed that includes the experience of adults living with dyslexia over a lifetime. An expanded awareness of dyslexia in the workplace and the compensatory elements that support a person's work would also be high on my wish list for future development.

I secretly hoped after graduate school I no longer would have to worry about dyslexia. My career and personal life have grown over the years in wonderful, surprising, and delightful ways. For me, it's been that 'Figure it Out' gene that I believe I have and suspect we all must have to one degree or another, that gets me through the rough patches each time. It is a magical combination of endurance, internal awareness, self-control, and an ability to see options and find joy in figuring it out.

Learning to laugh at oneself is an important skill. One time on a business trip, I checked a whole box of files on a flight to a city where I was going to spend a week working. When I was unloading the box from my car the next morning, I figured out I had grabbed the wrong files. I had misread the labels. I stood next to the trunk of my car and just chuckled. There was nothing I could do about it now; I just had to figure it out as I went along. Another time, I checked out of my hotel, drove to the airport, only to find out I was a day early for the flight. I had to laugh. No sense getting all worked up over it. I have been on stage speaking to an audience of healthcare professionals, and they heard me say an entire sentence backwards. Were it not for their chuckling, I might never have known I had made an error. These days, it's common to hear me ask someone, "Did that make sense?" It's not because I lack self-confidence; it's a way to check if what was in my mind came out accurately when I used my words. And when something didn't go as planned, I find my willingness to take it lightly a blessing.

I've gotten used to gently smiling or laughing at my goofs, and simply starting again. I've had a rock on my desk for years that is inscribed with the phrase 'Begin Again'. It's a reminder to return to the beginning of something, or to start where I left off. Either way, the sting of 'messing up' is eased both internally and externally. Be gracious with yourself and know that sometimes you just gotta laugh.

INTRODUCTION TO GEORGIE KOMEINER

Georgie grew up in Hungary and lived, studied, and worked in other European countries before moving to the United States. Georgie's success is built on a foundation of education and her ability to pivot; she has changed careers four times.

Georgie learned to balance work and life as a single parent and a graduate student without family support because they lived halfway around the world. She became a successful professional in the corporate world, and the critical moments and challenges in her life ignited her interest in coaching. As an HR professional, she helped people overcome workplace challenges and supported leadership to inspire and motivate their teams. Her experience has helped her realize that the only person who compromises our own confidence, is ourselves.

She is a professional certified coach, a mediator and senior HR professional, a Master NLP Practitioner, and a long-term user of the Silva Method which helps her guide this journey on earth more effectively. She is passionate about helping others in their holistic development. She believes that there is a success story inside of everyone. That story is waiting to be unleashed upon the world. Today, as mediator, a life and career transition coach, and a holistic leadership coach, Georgie helps others to create their own success stories in life, careers, and in their relationships.

STANDING TALL
Georgie Komeiner

Two years ago, during a weekend training session, one of the activities was to ask four of your loved ones to tell you why they love you and talk about your good attributes. I asked my seventeen-year-old daughter. I was expecting snarky comments, usual teenage sarcastic humor, but she described me as the most resilient person she has ever known and went on to describe me as her role model. I became intensely emotional. Intense, but good. I realized then that the voice in my head saying, *"I am not good enough"* and *"I am not smart enough"* was not right and was not serving me well. Here it was, unmistakable evidence that I am smart enough, good enough, and doing my best as a mom. This exchange was the first time I considered sharing my broader story.

There are so many wonderful women out there who spend too much time beating themselves up with self-diminishing talk, violating their own boundaries, and neglecting their own needs. Women extend themselves trying to fit in at school, at work, at their kids' school or any other communities, to prove to the world they are good enough, smart enough, pretty enough or whatever enough. I hope my personal story is inspirational to anyone who is struggling with these self-deprecating thoughts. Guess what? If I was able to get through rough situations, still move forward and achieve my goals, others can do that as well. I went from no job, sleepless nights, and considered suicide, and now I have a successful career that fully aligns with my core values and purpose.

My personal journey started as it does for most, in school. I grew up in the small country of Hungary in central Europe, where the school system does not support creativity nor individualism and squeezes everyone into a standard system and mold. Forty-five years of communism created an educational system which emphasized conformance and compliance. Still today, when students finish elementary school (elementary school is from ages 7-14), they are required to complete a standardized test which determines which secondary school they are eligible to attend. This was no different for me. At thirteen, with the pressure mounting, I had to figure out what I wanted to study and do. To be! Writing this now, I realize how insane this sounds. I did not feel good enough in any of the subjects, and I was not particularly interested in anything. I was still playing with Barbie™ dolls at age twelve. I had to figure out what school to go to, fill out applications, sit for a three-hour test, to get into the best school. Even with the pressure, I did well, and I got into one of the toughest high schools in the region. These years were the hardest in my young life, including my graduation studies in a foreign language and my professional certifications. Even with my exemplary test results and high grades, I still did not feel smart enough.

As my school years ended, my parents decided to separate after twenty-nine years of marriage. This came to me and my older sister as a barrel of ice on our heads. My dad never got over the divorce; he felt shame. During and after their divorce, he bribed and manipulated my sister and me and tried to turn us against our mom. Things I never imaged a parent would do to a child. He had become a different person. He was depressed, and verbal abuse was common, but I still loved him deeply. As the years passed, he became calmer and enjoyed spending time with his family again. Although he never recovered from the loss of his marriage, he didn't take any responsibility either. He blamed my mom until he passed. Thinking back, I realize he did not know any better. He did not know how to process the pain and grow from it.

I left. I left my home country to escape the pain of the abuse and heartbreak my dad suffered from. I was nineteen. I wanted to escape the family mess. The home that once felt safe, loving, and caring was now in ruins. I did not know what I wanted to study, but I knew I loved languages, and wanted to further expand my language skills. I became fluent in German and Spanish. I decided to start business studies while I figured out what was next and to learn English. English was easy; I was able to speak it fluently within three months. This amazed my teachers and my peers. It came naturally to me. My life was getting on track, despite the family drama between my parents.

Then I met the man of my dreams, John. Spending time with him helped my language skills immensely. I had someone to practice the new language with (he was American) and share my hopes with. He was generous, attentive, and affectionate. He seemed more mature than his friends and other guys our age. I felt very loved and safe around him. Although I strongly disliked when I learned he was an Army officer, my false beliefs about the military diminished as I learned about him, his culture, his work, and family. I fell in love with him deeply. I thought my life was in order. I started my undergraduate business/finance studies, and the vision of post-graduation started to take shape. Then things changed.

There was a tumor on my right ovary. They removed it, and I was in recovery when a fast-growing tumor was discovered on my left ovary. This was a blur of pain and fear. Healing was stunted because of my depression. I had no purpose. I thought to myself, *"What is my life worth if I have to drop out of school and never have children?"* I was twenty-one and thought there was no reason to live if I could not live the life I had imagined for myself. After weeks of despair, I chose to focus on getting well. I researched visualization techniques, herbal teas, and plant medicine supplements to rid my body of tumors. My grandma gave me a book from Maria Treben, and the inscribed message she wrote to me was *God gave us disease and illnesses but also gave us remedies.* I followed the Maria Treben guidance. I mixed my own teas and drank liters and liters of the herbal concoction daily. The second surgery was delayed due to holiday schedules. During the pre-operation ultrasound, the doctor was stunned when he could not find the tumor. There was nothing there. No tumor on my left ovary. Absolutely nothing. The doctor called his team into the exam room because he could not find it. I was confused because as he invited his entire team into the exam room, he did not tell me why. I was terrified because I thought it was worse than they initially thought. But it was the contrary. His perplexed face became happy as the other doctors confirmed there was no tumor anymore. When I saw his face change, I knew I did it. I conquered that nasty thing inside my body. I was healthy again. The surgery was cancelled, and now I have three children. Why am I writing this now? This was the first time I took control of my own destiny. I did not listen to my fear and pain. I wanted to prove I had power over my own life, and even my own health. Somehow, I knew I could heal myself, even though the doctors said I could never have children.

My husband was an army officer stationed in Germany, and we lived close to an American base. My eldest daughter was born quickly after our marriage. I had no help with my baby girl, but while she napped, I studied, preparing for an advanced test which would allow me to continue my studies at an American or English University. (All ESL, English as Second Language students are required to pass the test to study in higher education.) Military life was not easy, and then the Iraqi war made our life even more challenging. My husband was on a forty-eight-hour prep call, which meant he had to be prepared to deploy within forty-eight hours of notification. This status lasted for months. The threat of him being deployed seemed to last forever. My husband received orders to deploy in Iraq for a year. I was twenty-four years old. I had a young daughter and a baby boy on the way. I lived outside of my home country with no family nearby. The other women in my circle – wives and girlfriends of my husband's unit – did not have any children yet. When our husbands left, the wives and girlfriends returned to their home countries, and I was alone. Life was scary, isolating, and overwhelming. Weeks passed before I heard my husband's voice on the satellite phone to learn he was still alive. As my due date was approaching, I did get some help from my family members who started to come for short visits to help me out during those lonely days.

Even during deployment, John was preparing for his graduate studies and I for my undergraduate degree. When he returned home, we prepared to leave Germany, to spend time in Texas with his family, and then move to London where we planned to start our civilian life.

We landed in London, and life with two little ones was busy and fun. I found a job quickly at a conference center and proceeded to finish my undergraduate studies. I was determined to get my degree.

London is an extremely diverse place. People from all over the world live and work together in tight spaces. I remember this period fondly. I had good experiences at work and with my diverse colleagues. I had a female boss, with no children, and she too was studying for her degree while working. She was understanding, supportive, and was a great mentor. I was lucky she entered my life during this period. Our team consisted of people from all over the world, speaking all sorts of languages and English dialects. Since everyone was so different, I did not feel excluded. We were open and curious about each other's backgrounds, cultures, and experiences.

While my husband was finishing his MBA in London, he received a job offer in Hungary. It was a fantastic opportunity, and we decided to move to Budapest. He moved first, and I stayed in London with the children because I had to finish my semester of school. Once we settled in Budapest, I finished my bachelor's degree in Hospitality and Tourism Management remotely and worked for the largest conference venue in Budapest. The working environment was a culture shock, which is ironic given the fact I grew up in Hungary. I joined the sales team, and my colleagues were young single women with no children. The director who hired me left. Soon thereafter, two other employees left, and the whole remaining team had a lot to do but was untrained. We were required to work overtime without pay. At least I was close to family, and they became a supportive part of our lives.

While I was still working at the convention center, I began teaching ESL, mentoring on resume writing, and interviewing skills in English. I was eager to share my knowledge in English and job search skills. I found deep joy and pleasure in this work, and it gave me a sense of purpose. Helping others and passing on knowledge was rewarding, and still is. I secured my ESL Teaching Certificate from the University of Cambridge.

John's work involved international traveling, and I stayed home and taught English part-time. At the time, our children were in competitive sports which required practice every day, and commonly, there were tournaments each weekend. Life was busy, and I fell pregnant again without even noticing it. I did not think it was the right time, but John was not worried. He said we will figure this one out as we always do with everything. We are a team. A week later, while he was on a business trip, I lost the pregnancy. I felt guilty and ashamed. I blamed myself and thought it was my fault. I suffered with skin issues and went from doctor to doctor. Eventually, they discovered it was a hormonal imbalance. When I was healthy again, I told my husband I wanted to try and have another baby. We rested on the couch, and he turned to me with a smile, stroked my hair, and said, "We will have another baby. Miscarriages happen. Everything will be fine."

He was obsessed with materialistic things. He wanted fancy dinners, high-end hotels, and expensive gadgets. These were not as important to me, but since he was the primary breadwinner, I accepted the fact that he made the financial decisions for our home. He said his company wanted to focus more on the national market, and he might be able to earn more money in the United States. It would be beneficial for him in the states, and it would be easier to travel within the country. If he were traveling less, it would be a good opportunity for us to spend more time together, so I agreed to the move. He traveled frequently, but when he was home, we had a wonderful time together. Or so I thought.

We had spent summers in Texas. I was not scared, but I did not want to leave my family who lived near us in Hungary. I valued them after living in places with no family around. It was great to have my children around their grandparents, aunts, uncles, and cousins. Help was always available, even without asking. Our family values are strong. I was hesitant to leave that support behind and worried what it meant for my kids.

Before we moved permanently, we spent Christmas with my family in Hungary and stayed with my dad during the winter break. We flew to Texas on New Year's Eve. It was the last time I saw my dad. Ten days after we left, my dad passed away unexpectedly. The same day he passed, I discovered I was pregnant again. I returned to Hungary and buried my father.

Moving to the United States was tumultuous and started a whole new life for our family. A life I never imagined. We started our move to Austin, Texas. It seemed rushed. We bought a house too early, we moved in the middle of the school year, and I still had not gotten my visa. I was riddled with doubt, but John seemed confident, and since he made the money, I stayed quiet.

John was inpatient and frustrated. I thought it was stress associated with the move and the changes in his company. We eventually got everything settled at the new house in Austin. The kids and I spent the summer in Hungary. I was denied healthcare in the U.S. because of my pre-existing condition (pregnancy). We decided to have the baby in Hungary.

Two weeks before my scheduled due date, my life changed forever. Out of the blue, John abruptly told me did not love me anymore and that he wanted a divorce. He went on to say that he never really loved me and only married me out of a sense of obligation and duty. That if I had not been so pretty, he would have never married me. He insisted that I talk to a psychologist. I had no idea what was going on. I thought I was having a nightmare, but when I woke up in the mornings, the anguish was still there. He left. He took the kids to Austin. I was alone and about to have our third child. He came back to be with me when I had the baby. He spoiled me at a charming hotel, and it was a lovely weekend. I thought things were going to work out, that he still loves me and the children. We went to dinner two days before our baby was born, and he spoke about how different things would be for our new baby girl. She would have a different dad. I had no idea what he was talking about. I was mortified, confused, and hurt. My heart ached, and I squirmed inside. I thought our nice weekend together, his kindness, and the intimacy could only come from a loving husband, but I was wrong.

After my baby girl was born, he became cold and distant. It was awful. I felt so vulnerable and hurt, physically yes, but the emotional pain was unbearable. My c-section healing, I laid in bed with my baby next to me. I was disordered inside, crushed with confusion, and the betrayal manifested in physical pain. I fought my tears and tried not to cry with the fresh wound on my belly. I pretended that things were fine when visitors came. I said nothing to John who left for the night and came back to the hospital early the next morning smelling like booze and cigarettes. I stayed strong when I was the most vulnerable in my entire life. I saw happy couples and delighted moms with their new babies. I was devastated. I mentally prepared myself to get well quick to save my marriage and keep the father of my children. We got the little one's passport, and we were on our way to the USA and our new home.

I missed the other children terribly; they had started school in Texas while we had their baby sister in Hungary in early September. My mom came with me to Texas, and I was expecting the house and nursery to be in order. I had given John a list of items to arrange for our baby's arrival. After the grueling travel day, I was dismayed to find nothing prepared. There was no crib, tub, diapers, or changing table. There was nothing there for the nursery. He was anxious and fretting, easily angered. I was happy to see my older children, but John was someone else, someone new. He had a new practice of drinking every day. The liquor cabinet was his best friend, and he was always blurry eyed in the mornings. We tried therapy. One day, he would be nice and caring, the next he was annoyed and irritated by me and the children. It was a rollercoaster. I told him to leave and give us space. I had lost my father, had a baby, moved to a new country, and he was making our lives intolerable.

On Halloween, ten minutes before we were heading out for trick-or-treating, he ended our eleven-year marriage via text. He had someone new in his life and was sorry to hurt me. That was it. Trick-or-treating was a haze. The mask, the candy, the friendly neighbors. The kids yelling wildly as they ran from one house to the next. I pushed the stroller with my infant baby girl, dazed. One house had a party, and we were invited inside. I asked to go to a private room to nurse my baby, and as I was sitting on a stranger's bed, feeding my baby, my tears fell without stopping. I was embarrassed I knew no one. The months that came after are quite blurry, but I remember the physical pain that manifested from my emotional pain.

My husband filed for divorce and announced that he no longer wished to live in the U.S. He moved in with his girlfriend in the UK. He was living a double life for over a year or more. There were countless sleepless nights, painful days full of questions. How could he do this to me? He said I was a caring and loving wife, a wonderful mom to his children. He always said our family was the reason for his happiness. I did not understand the move, the super expensive anniversary gift, the lies about his travels. His credit card debt was ballooning, and he decided to leave it all behind, including me with the kids in the United States.

My second, and better, life started. He came back months later, asking for forgiveness and a fresh start. I was close to allowing him back in, but I realized the trust was so deeply violated, there was no going back. I also realized I deserved better. I was in a new country, over six thousand miles away from my friends and family. No career, no job, no friends, no family, no network in this country, but a baby and two small children who were depending on me. I talked to the only person I could, a therapist who charged me $180/hour. She discontinued with me after my husband threatened to get her license revoked because he found out that she gave me a family attorney's contact information.

I fell into darkness. I was in a dark hole. In the mornings, I managed to get out of bed, get the kids ready for school, make sure baby had time in fresh air, but then I went to bed because existing was painful. I had the thought that if I stayed in bed, life would stop hurting because I could hide from it. Six months of devastation and darkness threatened to consume me and my children.

Then one day, the light came back into my life. Hope. Seeking for meaning. Purpose. There must be a reason this happened. There must be a learning from this. We do not come to this earth to experience pain. We come to learn. When we are blind to the learning, life will guide us back on track. This might come with pain. Pain is inevitable in human life, but to suffer, especially for long, is our own choice. It is usually an unconscious choice. I made the decision to end my suffering and choose a life of hope and happiness.

I had no one to rely on, no one to trust. I had to create safety and stability for myself and my children. I stayed in Texas for my children. They started in a new country's school system only a few months prior. They were making new friends and were becoming better and better with their English. Taking them out of school and moving back to Europe would have resulted in them repeating a grade, and they would not have been close to their old friends. My priority was to provide them stability and security. Their father leaving was not only devastating for me, but for the kids too. They also faced his empty promises. There were forfeited visitations, and the things he said he would do with and for them, he never did. He moved to Europe and lived with his lover.

I had no idea how divorce works, especially in the United States. I had to figure everything out on my own. I learned legal language. I researched legal papers in the library. I did not have the means to hire a lawyer and was intimidated by my ex-husband. He had money and was a native English speaker; legal documents were easier for him to comprehend. But I kept reading and learning. I could learn anything. Anything. I think for first time in a long time, or maybe ever, I stood up for myself and made financial demands to my ex-husband. I could not afford to stay in the big house, and

I had no income to help me qualify for a mortgage. John's parents offered their second home for me to stay with the children so I could save money and find a new house. They supported me and advised me to get a good lawyer.

I created a plan. I prepared to solely support myself and the children in case John stopped helping us financially one day. I had to launch a career. My ESL teacher certificate would not get me too far not being a native speaker, and with three little children, I could not consider returning to the conference/hotel industry due to the schedule. I decided to apply for graduate school. I saved money and used some of my inheritance. I knew that my only option would be online or remote studying, and after researching the American universities which were too expensive, I applied to UK-based universities. I would take care of the family during the day and study at night. It felt like when I was young and venturing out on my own for the first time. I started my masters' studies in HR Training and Management.

As soon as I qualified for a mortgage, we moved into our new home, which was five minutes from my new job. The next two and a half years were busy. I was studying for graduate school while raising my children alone and fulfilling my work commitments. After a year of contract work, I looked for a position which aligned with my field of studies. I was able to secure a job, and I was responsible for hiring for various contract positions, facilitate HR related trainings, support leadership, and managing all employee relation matters. I had two wonderful managers. Two female leaders to whom I will always be grateful for their mentoring, leadership, and guidance.

They helped me gain confidence in my leadership skills and abilities, and they believed in me more than I believed in myself. Their confidence allowed me to recognize the greatness within me. I was concerned to let people know that I was a single mom with three children. I was afraid of the prejudice, that people would think I am less dedicated to work because of my family obligations. I will never forget a conversation I had with my manager after an overwhelmingly busy work week when I lost my patience and made snarky comments. She told me to show the real me at work. We are not only professionals, but some of us are also parents, some are students, some have interesting hobbies, and we come from diverse cultures and backgrounds. Sharing my vulnerability with co-workers, and other employees is a gift and creates closeness instead of distance. It builds trust.

This was when I began seeing my professional life through a different lens. The nature of my job in HR allowed me to see into people's lives, and I tried to help them. I became a good listener, whether it was a manager with their struggles or workers coming through my door. Ninety-five percent of the issues I dealt with as employee relations cases were because of miscommunication, assumptions, and misinterpretations, which rooted back into deeper issues. These issues, of course, were related to our basic core values.

I learned quickly that perception is reality and wanted to learn increasingly about human behavior. I still carried my traumas with me, and it unconsciously influenced every decision, action, and feeling I made or had. I wanted to learn more about myself and heal, and I wanted to help others to heal. I had regular meetings with my employees, and I did not understand how I could see their potential but they did not see it in themselves. Then I remembered my managers' voices: they believed in me more than I did, despite all my accomplishments. I realized that it is the same self-doubt our employees had. When I made my goals and laid out my plan during my divorce, I put the highest professional certification as my goal. I looked at what would qualify me to take the exam, and the shortest way was to get my master's degree which would reduce the requirement years to three years. I went for it and studied my butt off for these exams to become a senior certified human resource professional.

After reading countless books on self-development, leadership, human relationships, communication, and anything about human and organizational behavior, after taking numerous trainings to live my life in a conscious way, I want to pass on the knowledge and tell others: You are enough. You are perfectly imperfect as you are, as you are meant to be. I wish there were someone there for me at the beginning of my journey who held my hand through all the challenges life threw at me. But… then I would not be as resilient as I am now.

At the end, I would like to share things that helped me through my past challenges:

- Hurt people hurt people.
- There is no past, no future, we only live the *now*, so make the most out of it. It will never come back. Enjoy it now.
- Worrying is a waste of energy. Humans are afraid of the unknown. As soon as you get comfortable in unknown territory, you are empowered. And you can accomplish anything.
- There is trauma behind every person's defensiveness, mean actions, and behavior; it does not make it all right, nor do you have tolerate being treated poorly.

- The only real emotion or feeling is love. Every other feeling (fear, anger, frustration, loneliness, etc.) is created in our minds only. Change your thoughts and your feelings and actions will follow.

The moment my daughter told me I was the most resilient person she knew was important to me. Her words made me realize everything had been worth it. I knew the best way to help my children to get through tough times was to provide them with stability and teach them resilience. To show them that no matter what, they have me, and we would survive together. I will always be there for them, no matter what. My daughter is currently in technical training for her job at the Space Force. She is the only female in her class, but she is not intimidated in the male-dominated field. She is determined to reach her goals, and no one will stop her.

It was worth it. I am worth it. I am smart, resourceful, intelligent, resilient, and I can live my life just the way I want to. And you can too.

INTRODUCTION TO YALONDA BROWN

Yalonda J. Brown is committed to empowering others through her mission of embracing her divine purpose by improving the lives of others, especially women and girls. Yalonda currently serves as the President of Diversity Initiatives for Engage Mentoring in Indianapolis, IN. She holds a Master of Science in Organizational Leadership, and a host of certifications including being a Certified Child and Youth Care Practitioner. Whether it is via public speaking or her published works, Mrs. Brown uses her various platforms to inspire and motivate others to live according to their purpose. She is a seasoned professional with a host of accomplishments in both private and public sectors.

In addition to being an entrepreneur, Yalonda is a contributing author for several books. She is the author of

L.O.Y.A.L.T.Y.: A Girls Guide to Understanding Authentic Friendships, which reflects her passion for youth development and the empowerment of girls and women. She is currently writing and planning the launch of her next work titled: *L.E.A.D.E.R.S.- Learning to Engage Authentically and Develop Enriching Relationships in Society; A Curriculum for Girls on Navigating Relationships with Peers, Adults, and Community.*

A gifted speaker, she delivers powerful, dynamic speeches and workshops to diverse audiences. Topics range from youth development and overcoming obstacles to leadership, relationships, and faith. She aspires to use her voice to empower others. Yalonda is a highly sought-after leader, author, and public speaker. Collectively, her works inspire, build resilience, confidence, and character.

When she is not writing or speaking, Yalonda J. Brown enjoys spending time with family and friends, reading, shopping, and traveling. Yalonda is passionate about philanthropic interests and is active in her community.

She currently lives in Avon, Indiana, with her husband and daughter.

To learn more about Yalonda J. Brown, visit: www.justsayitllc.com

STAYING POWER: THRIVING IN THE STORM
Yalonda Brown

"Yalonda has demonstrated bravery and resilience by embracing the unknown with intention and joy."

I cannot share all my trials and triumphs, but the experiences over these past two years shook me to the core. When I look back at my weakest moments, I realize there is *no way* that I would still be here without God giving me new strength and lifting me up when I was fading. This faith gave me the confidence and resilience to not give up and the confidence to *rise* above the dire circumstances I faced.

The pandemic, for all of us, was punctuated with the national race-related unrest, unparalleled isolation, and unexpected lifestyle changes. My pandemic years included two surgeries, surviving COVID and multiple lingering health challenges, navigating the grief and solidarity alongside my husband during the quick and successive losses of my in-laws, maintaining productivity and execution of key deliverables at work, growing my personal business as an author, fighting my helicopter parenting tendencies of an adult daughter, completing a series of courses and certifications, and landing a high-functioning dream job reflective of my values and capabilities. These two years were full in ways I have never experienced nor could have predicted.

My story is not unique; women often take on the impossible and live to serve and support beyond our capacity. According to Webster's dictionary, staying power is the "capacity for continuing (as in existence, influence, or popularity) without weakening." This journey included unspeakable joy, and these principles are my mantras to achieving undefinable joy and resilience through the most difficult season of my life.

"What Yalonda's demonstration of bravery and resilience at work has meant to me is... the importance of understanding the ways we can SHOW UP. Being brave also means understanding YOUR voice and how you contribute in your own way."

L.O.Y.A.L.T.Y. Lessons for the Elevated Woman

- Love on yourself
- Reflect on who you are

- Practice gratitude
- Embrace your brokenness

Love On Yourself: Self-love is key to building resilience. Many of us, and particularly women, must learn the importance of loving themselves first, because only then can they love and serve others. L.O.Y.A.L.T.Y. stands for Loving on Yourself and Learning to Yield. (Brown Y. , 2019). As women, we nurture everyone around us and expend our energy. We must learn to yield to our own needs first and make self-care a priority. I had to learn this lesson about self-love especially during the pandemic when I had two unplanned surgeries. I realized the importance of being aware of my body and taking better care of my health.

Reflect: I relied heavily on prayer to seek the strength to endure the world spinning around me. I had to dig deep to reflect on how I wanted to show up for work, home, and the places I played, and prayed. I identified and then wrote down activities that brought me joy and made me feel good about myself.

Practice Gratitude: I was gifted a journal with prompts to indicate something each day for which I was thankful. This journal became a critical therapeutic tool, helping me to devote time each day to focus on thoughts of gratitude.

I had immersed myself into work, projects, and learning opportunities as distractions to mask my sadness.

Embrace your Brokenness: The journaling helped me realize I must embrace my brokenness. The world will tell us that brokenness means failure, but I would argue the strength we need as women, wives, mothers, or professionals only comes through brokenness. Grab a journal, a notebook, or even a scrap of paper and complete these sentences:

- Brokenness is……..
- I feel most joy in my life when……
- I create the best results in my life when…..
- I want the rest of my life to be about…..
- The kind of support I need more of in my life is…..
- The mask I hide behind/wear is……

Though I remain broken in an imperfect world, I developed an unwavering faith and confidence that I could rise above and manage through anything that came my way.

This can be your season of pruning. A garden requires pruning. Removing parts of plants, trees, or vines that are stifling the new and good growth are required for the greatest growth and beauty. Pruning eliminates elements that are harmful or stifling the health and development of the plant. In rose culture, pruning enhances a plant's shape and flowering potential, and new growth emerges. This was my season of pruning. Eliminating negative self-talk was required for me to survive and withstand the pain and challenges in my life.

It is important to find your own source of strength. For me, my source of strength is my faith in God that carries me through. I have never witnessed someone manage her transition from a vibrant independent being to the fragility caused by a cancer diagnosis that stole her life as gracefully as my mother-in-law. There were days I sat with her, she was in pain, and I whispered to her to "sing through the pain." She sang a verse of her favorite gospel hymn. I bore witness to her resilience and faith in action. It was hard seeing my husband hurt, to hear him cry, but he soldiered on after losing his parents in quick succession. I had to be strong for both of us. I redefined brokenness into an acronym to help me to stand firm during adversity.

B.R.O.K.E.N. Breaking, **R**emoving, **O**bstacles, with **K**nowledge, of God's Word, **E**vidence of His power, and **N**ever ceasing prayer. (Brown, 2016)

> *"God uses broken things. It takes broken soil to produce a crop, broken clouds to give rain, broken grain to give bread, broken bread to give strength. It is the broken alabaster box that gives forth perfume. It is Peter, weeping bitterly, who returns to greater power than ever."*
> **—Vance Harvey**

The pandemic, life, the whole series of events left me gasping for breath each day, each moment. A mentor shared this thought, "Don't be a victim, be a strategist." If you are a victim, then you only see the problems and challenges. You are reducing your own power as a victim, immediately reducing yourself and influence. A victory mindset sees opportunities and solutions and empowers the victor through the expectation of winning and capability. A victim uses excuses to quit, while an elevated woman finds ways to keep going, through the power of belief and firstly loving and caring for themselves. This was the compass I used as a coping and guiding principal throughout this time.

T.H.R.I.V.E. in the Storm

The pandemic stretched every fabric of my being. Yes, multiple illnesses, including COVID. Some people experienced mild cases of COVID – mine seemed mild, yet it carried lingering health challenges. It took me down, and I was in the storm! It does not come naturally to me to ask for help. I had to humble myself and let those who love me support me and my family. Why is it that some women balance the demands of marriage, motherhood, peer relationships, career, civic and community engagement, and so much more, with ease and grace? For every woman, the answer may differ as we each do what we must do to survive and care for those we love. There is hope and it is possible to thrive in the ebbs and flows of life. I have had to learn how to T.H.R.I.V.E.

T.H.R.I.V.E. Everyday

Time, **H**onesty, **R**elationships, **I**ntentionality, **V**ulnerability, and **E**mpathy (Brown, 2022)

Time

Life is short. How we spend our **t**ime reflects our values. Actions must be aligned with the desired results.

Honesty

I initiated crucial and honest conversations with my family, friends, and colleagues about my mental well-being and the societal unrest, racial tensions, and focus on diversity, equity, and inclusion. Between the incidents involving victims like Breonna Taylor, George Floyd, and Ahmaud Arbery, to being met with negative and fake news, I was not okay! I built my capacity for addressing topics around faith, race, and privilege. I facilitated conversations and saw relationships shift. I accepted that the pandemic shined a light on who was willing to do the heart work to maintain relationships, manage conflict, and learn how to respect and love authentically.

I became more aware and comfortable sharing my emotional triggers with others. This way, they knew what I needed and how to love me. My resilience was strengthened by my willingness to show up for others and in my ability to be still when my emotions began to overwhelm me.

Relationships

"What I love about Yalonda is that she was always brave enough to speak her mind, her truth, when it would benefit the greater good. But she was also brave enough to be silent. And resilient enough to defend both."

While life was taking an emotional toll, I was blessed to be a part of a team that was willing to lean in and do the work to build our capacity for discomfort, encourage questioning, embrace our differences, share our lived experiences, and develop an unbreakable bond of trust. Working for an organization where brave spaces were intentionally created for transparency and difficult conversations was exactly what I needed, and what we all needed. All of this helped build my resilience and willingness to remain a positive and productive contributor.

When I speak to young girls, I challenge them to consider:

Who is the girl I see? How is your self-esteem?

Who is the girl in my head? What is your self-talk?

Who is the girl others see? How are you showing up in the world?

The pandemic taught me that life is short, and I decided that it was time for a radical shift in how I managed relationships and how I showed grace and love to myself and to others. Ask yourself, if someone were to ask the five closest people to you about what you value most, what would they say? If you were to ask them how they see you, how close would their views of you match your views of yourself? I believe in creating legacy in all spaces I occupy. I remember standing up at my first staff meeting at an organization and stating in my introduction, "At the end of my tenure, you will know I was here." During the events of these past few years, it was important for me to show up brave and strong and lead with love while holding people in my life accountable.

It was not only important for me to hold others accountable but to also be held accountable. I encourage everyone to seek out a mentoring relationship. If it were not for organizations investing in my development, along with mentors who cared enough to nurture my potential and help me bring my best to each growth experience, I would not have been prepared for the opportunities I have been afforded.

It is one of the most amazing gifts to have someone speak into your life. I have often been asked, "Who are your mentors? Who are your role models?" There was a time when I would not have used the word mentor, I just recognized there were people who modeled behaviors for me that helped me be successful, grow, and learn. As a result of my maturation both personally and professionally, I began to understand that these were the mentors in my life. These influencers began with my grandmother and continued with teachers, ministry leaders, former colleagues, bosses, etc. I have had the pleasure of working with some of the most intuitive, smart, and insightful leaders who have groomed me throughout my career.

In a blog I read recently, the author states, "In this environment, I cannot discuss mentoring without talking about resiliency and I cannot discuss resiliency without talking about how important it is to connect with others meaningfully."

Authentic connections to others is a pillar to building resiliency. I was affirmed of my actions by what my colleagues shared.

"Yalonda has demonstrated bravery and resilience at work by embracing discomfort during challenging times and being intentionally open to understanding and celebrating the unique attributes of individual team members."

- How have you grown your relationships?
- What affirmations do you have in your life?

Intentionality

Every year for the past several years, I developed an annual mantra. In 2016, I vowed to "Live Boldly." I believe fervently that we must purposefully put forth the effort to achieve positive outcomes in our lives and feel and act in a way that promotes resiliency and exudes expectation. Other mantras in subsequent years were "Choose Joy!" and "Speak Life!" and "Be What You Want to See!"

- What is your mantra to achieve positive outcomes?

Vulnerability

"We can be our worst selves when we're afraid, or our best, bravest selves."[10]

This is a wonderful place for a mirror check. Being vulnerable, especially in the workplace is hard. There were days when I had to admit, I was feeling overwhelmed or that I had made a mistake or simply needed a wellness day off.

One of my former colleagues goes on to state, *"I have a clearer understanding of the depth of pain and the ways Yalonda was stretched over the last year and how she chose to carry it in the workplace. What she chose to share, be silent about, and how she chose to contribute and in what ways. The boundaries set, the barriers faced, and the behind the scenes "stuff" that showed the true depth of bravery and resilience she had to show up every day and to truly be joyful and steady through it all."*

- How have you demonstrated vulnerability?

Empathy

According to an article in the NY Times, "Mental health has become its own pandemic during the pandemic, with soaring rates of anxiety, depression, and burnout. But some studies show that a substantial portion of adults have found

---

10   www.ourmindfullife.com

ways to function and even thrive, despite dealing with the global health crisis and substantial upheaval." [11]

These past few years tested me. How was I to relate to the experiences and vulnerabilities of my colleagues when I was at my capacity? I honed my listening skills, practiced not always having to speak up, and asked others for their perspectives. It became important to me to hear and observe what was in the hearts of those closest to me. I became more patient with myself and others. I have had to learn how to T.H.R.I.V.E.

- How are you managing your mental well-being?
- How are you learning to T.H.R.I.V.E.?

Indescribable Joy

I wore my hustle and grind mentality like a badge of honor. My staying power and grit were the primary indicators of my resilience. The pandemic brought a new perspective to what it meant to bounce back from challenges and obstacles. I realized I had to make some radical changes in my life to tap into my faith for the strength needed to find joy.

God moved mightily in my life in 2021. The year began with my acceptance into an executive fellowship called *The Journey* where I was challenged to seek personal joy and renewal in the field of youth work. During the year, I attended

---

11   https://www.nytimes.com/2021/12/09/well/mind/emotional-resilience.html

four retreats introducing me to peace, fellowship, fun, stress relief, and the opportunity to get out of my comfort zone and just *be*. We create these mountaintop moments in our lives. I assure you, if you are not leading with renewal in mind by driving a culture that supports a comprehensive approach to employee wellness, you are not tapping in your team's full range of effectiveness or organizational commitment. I am a testimony that even when I was pushed to the point of mental and physical exhaustion, having a supervisor that supported my need to recharge helped me know I was valued.

Author Gail Wagnild states, "There is much accumulated research now that says if you can minimize thinking about the negative parts of your life, you will be more resilient. This doesn't mean that you delude yourself but rather that you learn to see hope where there is despair and discouragement. Knowing that we can experience joy during suffering helps us get through difficulties and makes life worth living. Envision joy as the light that dispels shadows. Think of it this way: If you can learn to see joy every day, doing so will go a long way toward helping you cope with the daily ups and downs of life."[12]

---

12   https://www.resiliencecenter.com/articles/healthy-and-resilient-aging/six-ways-to-more-joy-and-happiness-in-your-life/

I had to learn how to T.H.R.I.V.E. Each day, I had to make the decision to change my life, and you can too.

Each day, do this to change your life:

Have a Morning Affirmation: Say to yourself, "I will show up! I will thrive! I am enough!"

Say a Prayer: "Dear Heavenly Father, strengthen me to rise empowered with the spirit of resilience, grant me the clarity for my God-given ability to shine and the passion to glorify You in the midst of adversity. Amen."

You must find and implement a connection with what is good and meaningful for your life. Do this and you will T.H.R.I.V.E.

INTRODUCTION TO TRISHA TAYAN

Trisha Tayan is a human resources leader with over thirty years of experience in a variety of industries including technology, hospitality, logistics, pharmaceutical, and multi-industrials. Her HR areas of expertise are strategic human resource planning, talent development, performance management, succession planning, career development, organizational transformation, and leadership coaching. Always with a smile, she is passionate about being a trusted advisor and thought partner to executives and employees alike, helping them achieve their objectives and aspirations.

She received her master's degree in Management from New Jersey Institute of Technology, Bachelor's Degree in Communication and Human Resources Management Certificate from Rutgers University. She is a member of the Society of Human Resource Management and the International Coaching Federation. Trisha is currently pursuing a Professional Coach designation from the Institute for Professional Excellence is Coaching (iPEC).

Trisha lives in Pennsylvania with her husband and their two playful dogs. She enjoys traveling, spending time with family and friends, shopping, preparing meals, and sharing laughter.

Connect with Trisha Tayan on LinkedIn.

WOLF BITES
Trisha Tayan

Sitting at my desk, I stared at my swollen hands. They were tight, and the pain was excruciating. My hands were burning and were so constrained I could not hold a pen or make a fist. The pain made it hard to focus on work, and I could not pick up the phone or type. I was uncomfortable and wanted to go home and cry, like I had many times before. This hurt was not new to me but exceeded my previous experiences. My hands were not the only ones to suffer; my feet and joints ballooned, and I ached all over.

I had always been active, ambitious, and healthy. Each time my symptoms came, I had hoped they would go away. This time, sitting at my desk, I knew I couldn't take it any longer. I knew I needed to seek help. That day, right then, I called my physician and made an appointment.

I told the doctor about the pain, swelling, fatigue, and not feeling like my usual self. He reviewed my medical history and examined me. I was twenty-five and until recently been healthy and energetic. He said my symptoms could be related to a 'female issue'. *Really?* I knew my symptoms didn't have anything related to a 'female issue'. Despite his 'diagnosis', he gave me a referral to see a neurologist and to be evaluated for carpal tunnel syndrome. I made the appointment to see the neurologist. I suspected that I did not have carpal tunnel syndrome.

The visit with the neurologist included another medical history review and two tests that measured my nerves and nerve impulses. The neurologist reviewed my test results and concluded that I did not have carpal tunnel syndrome. She then referred me to an immunologist.

I didn't understand why she referred me to an immunologist. After Dr. Sullivan listened to my symptoms, reviewed my medical history and test results, she diagnosed me with undifferentiated connective tissue disease (UCTD). She went on to explain autoimmune disorders, and I was grateful that the neurologist referred me to Dr. Sullivan.

To relieve the pain and swelling, Dr. Sullivan prescribed a non-steroidal anti-inflammatory (NSAID) medication. When the first NSAID didn't work, she prescribed another, and then another. Since none of the NSAIDs provided any relief, she prescribed 20 mg of prednisone. After that first dose, the pain and swelling subsided. I finally started to feel like my old self again. No pain. No swelling. I could finally get on with my life and career.

As much as prednisone provided relief, like many medications, it came with a truck-load of side effects. Initially for me, the side effects were facial puffiness, otherwise known as moon face, mood swings, and increased appetite.

When I first experienced the symptoms of severe joint pain, swelling, fatigue, and learning about my diagnosis of UCTD, I worked for a company that sold Yellow Page advertising. Remember the Yellow Pages? I started there as an assistant to the Employment Manager. I was promoted because of the improvements I made to recruitment and advertising. I demonstrated my capabilities and willingness to learn and take on greater projects. I was developing in my career, and I was satisfied with my progression.

I took prednisone and still experienced symptoms periodically. I continued to see Dr. Sullivan and have regular bloodwork to monitor my condition. My test results showed inflammation in my body and then something else developed. One of the tests indicated that I might have Systemic Lupus Erythematosus (SLE aka Lupus) and another medication was added. Knowing that I would want to learn more about Lupus, Dr. Sullivan advised me to not read anything pre-1980s because all publications deemed SLE as fatal.

She explained that Lupus was an autoimmune disease where the body's immune system was overactive and attacked not only the bad cells but also the good cells in one's body. I learned that I had to stay out of the sun and to avoid people with colds, viruses, and other contagious diseases. I tolerated staying away from others with germs, but staying out of the sun was difficult to hear. Despite the pain, swelling, constant fatigue, multiple doctor office visits, tests, and various medications, I wanted to continue to work and grow in my career.

I felt lucky that the third doctor I saw diagnosed me with Lupus. In my research to understand the disease, I read stories of patients who sought medical attention for various ailments for years. Their doctors would treat their ailment, but the patients continued to be ill. These patients had to see several doctors, many more than three, before they were finally diagnosed with Lupus. Most patients suffered for years and years before being accurately diagnosed.

Managing my illness and continuing to work was something I learned over time. When I was diagnosed, I was in my mid-twenties and just starting my career. I was driven and didn't want this disease to slow me down. I didn't share my illness or struggles with anyone at work, and sometimes I even hid it from my family. I was afraid of what others might think or how they would treat me if they knew I had Lupus. I was worried I would be perceived as weak or incapable. I was worried how it would affect leaderships perception of me, and would I be strong enough to have a flourishing career. I scheduled appointments first thing in the morning or the last appointment of the day, to avoid missing work.

One day, after my second boss left the company, I drummed up the nerve to ask the head of the personnel department about what actions I could take to take on the next roles. He thought I should take a lateral move into sales, which would broaden my experience and prepare for the next level of responsibility. I understood his advice, but I was not interested in going into sales. I wanted to learn more about personnel, as it was called at that time; now we call it human resources.

While the prednisone provided relief, it was not permanent. I still experienced discomfort and swelling, sometimes in other parts of my body. One of my first flare-ups included a fever of 104°F. I was miserable and only wanted to sleep. My husband at the time, Chris, tried to cool me down with a bath, but it didn't work. Chris called Dr. Sullivan. She told him to take me to the emergency room immediately. I was in the hospital for several days. Tests were administered, doctors examined me and my history, and results were interpreted, but no certain cause for the flare or fever was identified. They concluded it must have been Lupus-related, and I was discharged and ordered to stay home for recovery and rest.

Since I was not good at sitting still while I recovered and was not happy about the career advice, I took the opportunity to look for another job. After a couple of months of looking, I found something with more responsibility and higher pay.

My new job was an HR Assistant for a business unit of a Fortune 500 company, and I loved it. I was the only HR person for the business unit, but I operated with support and guidance from a manager who was in another state and seasoned colleagues who were onsite supporting other business units. I learned and grew so much in that role and at that company. There were new experiences, and I was progressing in my career.

While I was in this role, I did not share my diagnosis with anyone. I was afraid. I feared I would be treated differently, and I didn't want anyone to feel sorry for me. I was fearful of the stigma of illness, especially an illness that people did not understand. At that time there were few outward signs of my illness, and people would not believe I was ill. Hiding my illness was a lie. It was hard to maintain the lie, and the longer I hid my disease, the heavier the burden of lying about it grew.

In addition to the day-to-day struggles with pain, swelling, fatigue, and side effects of medications, and the plethora of doctor visits required for treatment, I experienced two lupus flare-ups while at this company. One was pancreatitis, and the other was a severe skin rash. Neither of those flare-ups required hospitalization, and I hid them. I hid them because that was the lie I chose to live.

The pancreatitis was uncomfortable with crushing abdominal pain. It caused frequent trips to the bathroom. The treatment for pancreatitis required medication and diet changes. The pancreatitis eventually faded and then I was hit with the skin condition. The severe skin rash was the result of sun exposure. I loved the sun! Even though I was not supposed to be exposed to too much sun, my vacation back home to Hawaii was magnificent. I spent too much time in the sun, and the result was a severe skin rash. The rash started small but eventually covered my body. It was unrelenting pain, and my skin peeled off me. Wearing clothes was extremely uncomfortable, and it was hard to ask for the help I needed to apply cream that treated the rash.

Despite my debilitating discomfort, I continued to push myself, putting my work and career first. I was promoted several times and earned my MS in Management.

After I earned my MS degree, the business unit I worked for started discussions about relocating to Raleigh, NC. It was the impetus I needed to make a career change. I wanted to try on new opportunities in a different industry. My new job was in a new location, and I moved to the greater Philadelphia area.

The first years were great. I worked with great people, I had challenging projects, and I was traveling. The work and travel requirements began to take a toll on my health. My lethargy and soreness became constant, and my doctor advised to take a break from traveling.

I enjoyed my job and did not want to leave. Fortunately, my boss was understanding and accommodating and helped me find a role that did not require travel. I was in that role for a year, and it gave me the opportunity to learn and develop expertise in employment policy and practice, and learn about my body, heal, and care for myself. Since I was feeling better, I wanted the next promotion and wanted a role that included travel. I applied to and was hired for a role in Training and Organizational Development. I loved that job, the work, my team, and my boss.

me that since I wasn't considered to be her successor, she would have to let me go. *What!?* I could not believe it and did not understand. The news about how I was viewed, and my impending termination was wholly unexpected. My performance was never an issue. I was floored. We negotiated a long separation timeline to give me time to find a new position. The long separation period became awkward and made it more difficult for me to let go of my work.

During the next three years, I did project work and landed a job at a company in Maryland. Within a year with the company, my kidney function decreased. Every time I went to the nephrologist, my results were poorer and poorer. Finally, my nephrologist recommended my placement on the transplant list to build time. Due to my blood type, we expected a 6-8 year wait for a transplant. I had to consider the type of dialysis I wanted, and I was sent home with a pile of pamphlets and a DVD to learn more.

The transplant planning was easier than evaluating the dialysis types. I couldn't face it. I burst into tears every time I thought about being on dialysis. My lab results, level of fatigue, weakness, and lack of appetite forced me to select a dialysis treatment type. I decided on peritoneal dialysis so I could administer the treatment myself and continue working performance management cycle, and I couldn't bear the thought of not working on this project. In my condition, I could not lead the effort full-time from the office. I asked my boss if I could run the project from home. She agreed, and the vendor and our HRIS manager even came to my house for project meetings. It is amazing what happens when you share your struggles and ask for help. People want to help.

As physically weak as I was, my mind and spirit were still strong. Being able to work on the project and contribute helped me heal along with the multiple medications, chemo treatments, blood transfusions, and my strong will to heal. I believe meditation, my mindset on healing, and being grateful to recover from my kidneys on the brink of failing also helped my healing.

Months went by before I was able to return to the office. When I did return, I started part-time and worked on building back my strength. While I appreciated being back, I felt different about my priorities and how I was going to live my life going forward. I still had to go to doctor and lab appointments, but I no longer hid those things from anyone at work.

One late afternoon, almost six years after being in the hospital, I was working late. As I got ready to leave, my boss asked to speak with me. We went to her office, and she told of sorts. I knew I was not well, but I had soldiered on; now I might have to be on a transplant waiting list.

I was miserable and simply wanted to go home and get well. I was tired, had no appetite, no energy, and was depressed. It was difficult to eat; I was not hungry, but the doctors stressed that I needed nutrition. Nothing tasted good, but I forced myself. My sister brought me healing meditations, and this practice began my path to healing. Meditating helped with flare-ups, especially to focus on something when the pain was extreme. I was determined to get better and get out of the hospital.

Finally, after two weeks, my kidney function started improving, I began to feel better, and a ray of hope opened up. By the end of the third week, I went home. I was still weak, weighed less than 100 pounds, and I was advised to not drive. Thankfully, my mom lived nearby, and she helped get the 20+ prescriptions, took me to appointments and treatments, and made sure I had everything I needed to be comfortable and heal.

Right before I was admitted to the hospital, there was a project at work I had initiated. I was eager to get back to it and drive it to completion. The project required designing and implementing the company's first online performance management system. The timeline aligned with a new and they admitted me immediately. An array of doctors ran tests and questioned me. As time passed, I felt worse with increasing weakness, fatigue, and lack of appetite.

After being admitted to the hospital and since I was supposed to be on vacation, I thought I would be treated and be better by the end of the week and then return to work after my 'vacation', and no one would know what had happened. I had Lupus nephritis.

The hospital I was admitted to didn't have the proper treatment options, so I was transported to another hospital in an ambulance. After the first week in the hospital, I was not better. I could not return to the office in this condition. I had to tell my boss that I would not be in. Even though I was not required to tell her why I was not coming in, I felt obligated to explain myself. It was hard to make that phone call and tell her. Once I told her, I was relieved. I did not have to hide my illness any longer.

Two weeks in the hospital with an array of treatments, medications, blood transfusions, and plasma pheresis, and still my condition did not improve. We discussed the possible need for dialysis and kidney transplant. I had read about other Lupus patients having flare-ups that affected their kidneys but never thought I would be one of them. It was an awakening the doctors said it, I suspect the treatment of vasculitis caused early menopause.

Unfortunately, that job only lasted two years. In between jobs, I consulted, then landed a position as a director. A year into my director title, I was promoted into the VP level. I was thrilled. I felt accomplished and in the right place in my career. There was so much work to do, and I enjoyed every minute of it. Despite my ongoing health challenges and how I felt physically, I was energized about the work. I was engaged, worked long hours, and growing my career continued to be a priority. After a couple of years into the role, I became more tired than usual, and my nightly sleep was not restful. Every morning was a challenge and as was my practice, I tried to push through. Get out of bed. Get ready for work. Drive to work. Work. Work. Work. I knew I was faltering, by now I knew the signs, and a vacation with my sister was looming. I thought the vacation would help me rest and recharge. I went to the doctor the Friday before, to get in a check-up before we left. I shared my symptoms, and she ran a urinalysis. After seeing my results, she sent me to the emergency room.

I stopped by my house, made a couple of calls to let my family know what I was doing and that I most likely wasn't going on the trip, then drove myself to the emergency room

Next on my list of health challenges was vasculitis, which is the inflammation of the blood vessels. For me, the inflammation caused the vessels to burst and resulted in painful blisters all over my body. I had to wear loose-fitting clothing and clogs or mules. On rainy days, I covered my feet in plastic to avoid the blisters from getting wet. I kept working out of necessity, and it helped take my mind off the agony I was experiencing. Having vasculitis and the blisters was the most painful year of my life. I still have blister scars dotting my body.

The treatment for my vasculitis flare-up included an increased dose of prednisone, an immunosuppressant, and cortisone pulses. After I eventually healed from the vasculitis, I started having hot flashes, even though I was only forty. It was embarrassing to have a burning sensation rush over me while I sat at my desk or tried to chair a meeting. Thankfully, the first time it happened, there was a mall nearby where I went to get a change of clothes because I sweat completely through my clothes. These were not normal hot flashes; these were severe waves of heat that I could not hide from the person sitting next to me. My doctor tried a range of treatments to alleviate the hot flashes, but nothing helped. Over time, the extreme hot flashes decreased. While none of vs. going to a dialysis treatment center multiple times a week and interrupt my work schedule.

I had to tell my boss that I needed time off from work for a week to recover from a dialysis catheter placement in my abdomen. I also had to tell her that I would need intermittent flexibility and time off from work for three weeks to learn how to administer the dialysis treatment. That conversation went better than I expected; she and the firm were supportive of my healthcare needs.

After I recovered from the catheter placement and learned how to administer the peritoneal dialysis, it took several months to get used to having dialysis as part of my daily routine. Each evening, I set up the treatment, then administered it. The process took nine hours each night. Each morning, I had to clean-up, get ready for the day, and hustle to work. The dialysis helped, but I still was frequently fatigued. No matter how much I slept, sleep was not restful because I was doing an overnight dialysis treatment.

A few months after I started dialysis, a recruiter contacted me about an interesting opportunity in Delaware. I decided to pursue the opportunity and after interviewing, I was offered the role and accepted.

At the first team meeting with the new company, we introduced ourselves with a collage. I took this opportunity to include my health challenges with my teammates instead of hiding as I had done for so long. I overcame my fear and found the courage to share my story. It felt good to not lie or hide my story. Everyone I worked with at the new company was welcoming and inclusive. The work with my client group was challenging and satisfying. The organization was in the process of redefining itself. I excelled at the planning and execution of change management for the company. The organization changes continued, and I was affected. In two years, I had four different bosses. While I enjoyed collaborating with my new boss, I had a sense of loss when responsibilities were shifted to someone new, and it felt like a demotion. The onset of COVID racked our world, and HR responsibilities changed overnight for the whole firm. Each day, we were discovering and developing new ways to manage our workforce and pivot to remote work environments.

On a sunny Sunday afternoon, I got the call for a kidney match. I was excited but nervous that it would fall through. The transplant coordinator asked if I was ready. Of course, I was ready! I would do anything to end the dialysis. Blood types and other basics were checked, then he asked me to come in for final testing.

My sister and I arrived at the hospital around 4:00 p.m., and I was put in a patient room, had a COVID test, and more blood drawn. The nurses and doctors hustled in and out, peppering me with questions and updates. Time seemed to slow and expand. We had to wait. Wait for COVID results. Wait for blood results. Wait for the kidney to arrive. Wait for the surgeon to approve. Each step, each test was another opportunity for a failure. For me to be rejected. For the transplant to not proceed. Through all my research, I knew it was uncommon for patients to be rejected or sent home at the last minute.

After four hours of waiting and preparing for surgery, orderlies appeared with a gurney to wheel me down to the operating room. My sister gave me a big hug, and they wheeled me away. I arrived in the pre-op room and met the anesthesiologists, the surgical nurses, and the surgeons. They explained the anesthesia, the surgery, started the anesthesia, and moved me to the operating room. The cold room pulsed and faded. My eyes slid over the face of the doctor and landed on the box that held my new kidney. Then I was out.

I woke up groggy. The recovery room was chilly, but I was tucked into a warm blanket. Was this real life? Did I have a new kidney? In the early morning hours, I was returned to my hospital room. The on-duty nurse woke me up with a crisp schedule for the day which included a visit from the surgeon, the transplant team, and a physical therapist.

I couldn't get out of bed, let alone walk. However, with the help of the physical therapist, not only did I get out of bed, I walked out of the room and halfway down the hall and back. I used a walker, but I did it! The physical therapist made me sit in a chair instead of crawling back into bed. It was incredible how getting out of bed and walking around was part of the healing process.

I was in the hospital for a week. Every day, I was grateful for receiving a new kidney, especially because it was three years earlier than expected. I transitioned home after a three week stay at the at the Gift of Life Family House. The doctor expected me to be able to return to work within three to six months after the transplant. With the rate of my improvement, I couldn't imagine that my recovery would take that long. After two months, I felt ready to return to work. My doctor gave me his blessing as long as I could work from home. I had to be careful with the raging COVID pandemic. I was taking an anti-rejection drug and an immunosuppressant to prevent rejection of my new kidney, making me high-risk.

Two months after my transplant, I returned to work. My company and my management were accommodating. I eased back into part time and partial workload. Within eight weeks, I was full time and full workload.

The healthcare appointments and management did not go away but did change. I no longer had to do the dialysis treatments. The difference between dialysis and a functioning kidney is hard to describe. The quality of life with a new kidney was off the charts compared to living life on dialysis. The fatigue, chronic lethargy, and depression were gone. I literally had a new lease on life, not just in duration but in the quality of life I now got to live. I still have a heavy healthcare burden in my life, continuing with the anti-rejection and immunosuppressant, and I have to eat a balanced, low-fat, low sodium diet. But the world seems brighter, more energized, more exciting now. I almost feel as like I did before my diagnosis when I was twenty-five.

When I look back over the 30+ years I didn't feel well with chronic fatigue, pain, swelling, anxiety, insomnia, side effects of medications and treatments, hiding my illnesses, various flare-ups, and dialysis, I now see that stress contributed to the cause of the flare-ups. Learning how to deal with and manage chronic illness happens in real-time, with real people, all around us. We do not know what the person next to us on the subway or our colleague in the next cube is struggling with. I am thankful that I finally stopped hiding my illness and sought the support of my employers and friends. It was a critical decision in my ability to get and stay well. Even with a chronic debilitating illness, I have a successful career of which I am proud. I have achieved the goals I have set out to achieve, and I have new journeys to pursue. I have the endless love and support of my husband and family, and I am forever grateful. I am a determined woman with a lifetime of learning to share with the world.

Critical things I have learned:

1. Ask for help. Your family and friends want to help you be successful, happy, and fulfilled.
2. Establish priorities. Health and well-being are my priorities because without them as a foundation, I cannot do what I want to do in this lifetime.
3. Be willing to share the struggles you are experiencing.
4. Know the difference between healthy and unhealthy stress management. Adopt healthy means for managing stress.
5. Take deep breaths and meditate.
6. Give yourself grace and eliminate the concern about what others think of you. Beating yourself up does not serve you.
7. Relax and rest. It's needed to rejuvenate mind and body.

8. Acknowledge any illnesses, seek treatment early, learn how to manage the illness, and focus on healing.
9. Mindset is powerful. It can help or hurt any situation.
10. Know when to push yourself and when to rest and recharge.
11. Keep a sense of humor and remember to have fun.

The best way to start each day is to be thankful for the blessings in yourself and in your life. Then go and be who you want to be!

INTRODUCTION TO HOPE MUELLER

Hope Mueller is a pharmaceutical executive and author. Her early years were a crucible of hunger, violence, and drug use. Today her life is full of abundance and joy. Hope's story is inspiring, terrifying, and bold.

Hope is the author of two inspirational memoirs, *Hopey* and *Counting Hope*. She has published a guided journal, *Become,* and several articles. Hope is the founder of Hunter Street Press, a boutique publishing company focused on motivational material that positively impacts readers. Hunter Street Press offers line editing, co-authorship, and strategic story telling services to aspiring authors. Through Hunter Street Press, ambitious authors achieve their dreams of publication.

Hope is ardent about giving back, and after multiple charitable board seats and community outreach programs, she founded Hunter Street Charity and the Mueller Scholarship. Hunter Street Charity assists children and families during critical junctures in their lives. The Mueller Scholarship funds high school students who have suffered a catastrophic event and persevered through graduation and are entering college.

Hope splits her time between Northern Illinois, Tennessee, and Nevada. She is a voracious reader, dabbling artist, and an avid thrill seeker. She loves traveling, exploring, and relaxing with her best friend and partner, Brad Mueller. Hope is proud of the strength and confidence of her four daughters and grandsons.

Connect with Hope:
Facebook: Hope Mueller, Author
Twitter: @hpmueller242
Instagram: @hpmueller242
LinkedIn: Hope Mueller
www.hunterstreetpress.com
www.hunterstreetcharity.com
www.hopey.net

ONLY SPEAK WHEN SPOKEN TO
Hope Mueller

"Only speak when spoken to." Geoff instructed. "Don't talk in any meeting unless you are asked a direct question." He paused. I heard his breath through the phone because I was holding mine. "And don't offer an opinion."

Geoff knew what he was talking about. Being quiet and not contributing was what the company, this division, and this leadership, wanted from me. I was floored. I was promoted to the divisional level a few months prior with the promise of an increase in pay, bonus, and title. The pay and bonus came immediately with the promotion, but the new title did not. This was my mid-year review with Geoff, and I was prepared to discuss the new title. I was unprepared for the guidance Geoff was providing.

I had been responsible for leading continuous improvement (CI) at a manufacturing site. We were successful in several areas, and the VPs of the division noticed the achievement, which prompted the promotion. My responsibilities grew from leading CI for a single 24/7, 9-line, parenteral facility, to driving continuous improvement for eight global sites at the divisional level.

I gulped down my frustration and asked, "When can I expect the new title?"

"Well," Geoff hesitated. "We are not going to be able to proceed with that right now."

The feedback from the leadership team of the division was that I was overly confident and worked too quickly. I needed to slow down. Build consensus. And only speak when spoken too.

I was confused, hurt, and angry. I knew Geoff heard the catch in my throat and the tears stinging my eyes because my voice wavered. I got the promotion six months prior, and it required a re-location to Northern Illinois. The move was tumultuous and near devastating for the structure of my single parent home. There was no family support, few friends, and the change for my fifteen-year-old had proven too much. And now I could only speak when spoken to at work.

The worst part was, he was right. He was right and it was maddening. He knew what it would take for me to be successful with this leadership team, in this division, at this firm.

What is the value in squelching your power and capability? What is the value in shrinking yourself? It depends on the environment, the culture, and the contribution you want to make.

Everyone in corporate America must code-switch, and commonly for women and minorities, a method deployed is to diminish ourselves, our roles, our contributions, and even our speech. We squelch ourselves in our language: 'does that make sense?', 'I know I am probably wrong but', and the overused 'this is just an idea but'. We keep quiet and are careful not speak too much, too loudly, or too often. Although there is an assumed common knowledge that women speak more than men, work is being done to dispel this misconception. In a study of 155,000 company conference calls over nineteen years, it was found that men spoke 92% of the time.[13] On average, women speak 25% less than men in meetings when men and women are present.[13] And men perceive discussions as 'equal' when women spoke about 15% of the time and

---

13 Gender Inequality in Deliberative Participation, Christopher Karpowitz et al, Cambridge University

the discussion was being dominated by women if they talked only 30% of the time.[14] Does the perception create the reality, or is reality reflected in perception? Only 30% of *speaking* characters were female in the seven hundred top grossing films from 2007 to 2014.[15] The fact is women are not allowed to speak as often as men. And if women speak anywhere between 15 to 30% (or more) of the time they are perceived as talking too much or dominating conversations.

These numbers are shocking. We, both males and females, have room to grow, and we must consciously strive to improve this reality. Men have a blind spot, and their awareness and perception does not match documented reality. I surmise that what I experienced was not solely because I am female, but it was a contributing factor. An aggressive, confident young male would not have been told he was 'overly confident' or instructed to 'only speak when spoken to'. In fact, if I had been male, I may have received the opposite guidance and my promotion would have been swift and complete with the title offered.

Starting early in life, the guidance and expectations for girls and boys is different. My youngest daughter, Lauren,

---

14 Learning to Lose: Sexism and Education, Dr. Dale Spencer
15 Inequality in 700 Popular Films: Examining Portrayals of Gender, Race, &LGBT Status from 2007 to 2014, Smith Stacy L et al, USC Annenberg School for Communication and Journalism

plays basketball. There is a talented, dominant player on the team, and the remaining players are solid. This group of girls are a decent team, and they win frequently. There are times when they are ahead of the opposing team by twenty or even thirty+ points. When this is occurring, the most-talented player is coached to ratchet it back. She is told to take less shots, steals, and make fewer blocks. She is instructed to give the other team a chance and to consider how the other team members feel. Young male players aren't given this same coaching. They are taught to 'finish the game' and to not let an opposing team 'back in the game.' This is especially true for talented, dominant male players. Male players aren't told to decrease their efforts or slow down. As a kid, how often was Lebron James told to take less shots? Coaches don't tell male teams to worry about how the other teams feel. Talented young male basketball players don't suppress their power and capability; they are encouraged to lean into it and develop a killer instinct. We need to do the same for females.

For the young, dominant lady on Lauren's team, I challenge the guidance she is given. I tell her to lean into her talent, play hard, and develop her killer instinct. When the opponent is down, you make sure they cannot come back and win. If she wants to play Division One (D1) in college basketball and continue to dominate, she needs to hone her craft. At this critical time in her development, 6th grade, she should not be cultivating ways to slow down or diminish her ability. She should not be concerned about the other players' feelings.

We wonder why male and female D1 and professional basketball is so different to watch. Ultimately, it is a different game because of how the two genders are coached early. Females' killer instincts aren't developed until later in their basketball careers. By then the drive to win is muted, and these female athletes must unlearn what they were coached to do for their first few years of playing. They were being taught to slow down, take less shots, and to worry about how the other players felt. This same phenomenon happens in business and is what I experienced when I moved to Northern Illinois. Women are not encouraged to lean into their strengths or be confident and decisive until much later in their careers.

Not only are women not allowed to speak, but women are barely expected to exist. Although women make up just over 49% of the global population, females make up 17% of the average 'crowd' in movies.[16] Two-thirds of all central characters in children's books are male, and a character appearing in a title is twice as likely to be a male one.[17] These

---

16   Gender Stereotypes: An Analysis of Popular Films and TV, Smith Stacy L et al, USC Annenberg School for Communication
17   Gender in Twentieth-Century Children's Books: Patterns of Disparity in Titles and

numbers directly correlate to what we see in corporations around the globe. In 2022, women make up 19.7% of the global board members.[18] Women hold 25% of the five critical C-Suite positions.[19]

This is a staggering phenomenon. If there are more than 20-30% females in crowd scenes, viewers perceive the film to be dominated by women. These ratios are about the same for speaking. If women speak more than about 20% of the time, men feel that women dominate the conversation. Does the perception create the reality, or is reality reflected in perception? Is it because these ratios are what we have seen in media and entertainment for so long, or is media and entertainment a reflection of societal norms and expectations?

How do we change this paradigm? How do we improve this? Females are ~50% of the population but can only show up or speak about 20% of the time without people perceiving that we are too strong or contributing too much. We must find ways to have honest conversations with our colleagues and partners about these stark truths. The first step to any healthy change is to understand and accept the reality that exists today. Research the statistics, research the data, be armed with information. Then let's show up. When given

---

Central Characters, McCame Janice et al
18   Women in the Boardroom, 2022 Update, Konigsburg and Thorne, Deloitte
19   Korn Ferry Analysis of the Nations 1,000 Largest U.S. Corporations, Jane Stevenson

the chance to take a seat at the table—take it. Do not take fewer shots or less steals. When invited to contribute, do that. Contribute wholly and honestly and to the best of your ability. And finally, bring others to the table with you. Make sure the teams you build and participate within are diverse. Demand and implement diversity in all areas of your life and sphere of influence.

The data is on the side of diversity. "Companies with a higher proportion of women in decision-making roles continue to generate higher returns on equity while running more conservative balance sheets."[20], states the Credit Suisse 2016 Report. The report then goes on to say, "in fact where women account for the majority in the top management, the businesses show superior sales growth, high cash flow returns on investments, and lower leverage."[20] Winning and improving business lies in generating, promoting, and developing diversity—male, female, and minorities. Diversity of thought generates the best ideas to drive better business decisions.

No one should tolerate this inequity, especially in the light of the real benefit to businesses when women are in critical decision-making roles. Shrinking doesn't only impact and is expected from women, some men must deploy these

---

20 The CS Gender 3000: The Reward for Change Credit Suisse 2016 Report

tactics too. Unless they are on the sideline of a football field, minority men are expected to adjust their style, their voice, and even their stature to be heard and be successful in corporate settings.

Cohort 122, Kellogg Northwestern, was assembled in the large auditorium to hear two alums speak about their success. A female and male African American. The presentation allowed them to share their journeys and the audience then asked questions. For me, the most striking part of the presentation was the stark difference in which the two alums presented themselves. The female was strong, loud, outspoken, and oozing confidence. The male too was confident, but it was measured, not overt. His voice was low, almost monotone, and we had to strain to hear him. He rested on a tall stool, slightly hunched, making his body smaller. He smiled easily and was patient when she answered the audience questions first, and he waited for his turn to speak. This moment. This view. These two people. Each successful unto themselves, but this man had to mask, had to adjust, to be heard in corporate America, and I suspect in the world. He literally had to be small. He shrunk his body and voice. To achieve his success and to secure an SVP title, he had to be less. When are we going to allow Black men to be confident, loud, and stand tall in an office setting? This man had to adjust himself to gain success, he could not be intimidating, self-assured, or bold. I was impressed with both speakers and thankful we heard their stories. The difference in their presentation and delivery was so obvious to me, I realized that women are not the only ones who have to diminish themselves to achieve their dreams.

These are the hard facts of our own willingness to make ourselves small. To reduce our contribution. To own our voice. I am an SVP in the pharmaceutical industry. A role I drove hard towards achieving and here I am, still unlearning the habits that reduce my contribution. The tools and techniques I deployed to accomplish this position were service-oriented. I had to make myself submissive and useful. I took on operational and coordination tasks, proving the volume of work I could complete and deliver. I raced around ensuring the men, and women, in my sphere were prepared, informed, and ready to lead. My career is littered with examples of managing my bosses' budgets, preparing materials for their day, and ensuring they were set up for success. Corporate America is filled with women managing calendars, schedules, coordinating events, and important meetings. Meanwhile, the executives show up and opine. The burden of managing and coordinating tasks and calendars reduces our ability to strategize, stretch our ideas, be decisive, and lead. We are too busy making sure everyone got the meeting invite, is on the call, and they are well prepared for us to contribute our ideas and opinions meaningfully. The data proves that companies benefit when women and diverse teams have a seat and a decision-making voice at the table.

In our effort to secure critical decision-making and power roles, I, and many women, play support roles.[21] These roles get us close, but not quite, into the C-Suite. Everyday common roles for women include the ever-favorite Mom role. Or the Operational Support role for the leaders in an organization, commonly men. It is what got me here, but these tactics and activities will not help me attain the next level. At this level, I must do the opposite to be successful and to contribute meaningfully. I cannot offer to schedule meetings, build slide decks for others, or coordinate events. I must stop asking if something I said, 'makes sense'. How often do men discuss something or offer an opinion, then ask, 'does that make sense'?

I am almost fifty and am still unlearning these behaviors. I overuse the phrase 'This is just an idea, but'. I lessen my input with 'this is outside my area of expertise, but.' My least favorite phrase I have used is 'I know this is crazy' or 'I

---

21 We're your colleagues- not your mothers, Lexy Marton, Fast Company, Strong Female Lead 06-29-21

know I am crazy, but.' Reducing my words and contribution no longer serves me. I cannot diminish my opinion because it makes me a less effective leader. Like the talented, young female basketball player who will have to unlearn squelching her killer instinct, I must unlearn the techniques I used to get to this level. My notebooks and desks are cluttered with reminders to quit making myself small and that my contribution is valuable. Not bringing my full self and my full voice to the table erodes the perception of my competence. And, importantly, does not serve the business.

When I lead and participate, I make a positive impact on the business. Apologizing or putting myself in a submissive position lessens me and decreases the positive impact I make on and for the business. The note on my desk right now says this: Quit making yourself small and submissive, it no longer serves you or the company.

The only way to change these realities is to accept our role in our own demise and be willing to bravely step forth with strong voices, with partners and sponsors who are committed to real change. "You must be the change you wish to see in the world." Gandhi. We all must adjust our styles to meet people where they are. We must find ways to make space for people; for whom they are and how they show up. There is a space and a success for each of us. We own ourselves. We own our voices. When we gain leadership roles, we must demand diversity, inclusiveness, and equal pay. We must make room for the strong Black men. We must make room for bold women. We must be the change we want to see in the world.

What is the value in squelching your power and capability? What is the value in shrinking yourself? It depends on the environment, the culture, and the contribution you want to make. Of course, you could make yourself small, you can find comfort in not contributing, if it fits your needs and the life you want to live. Finding ways to honor yourself, and your inner voice, will unleash your fullness and a happiness unparalleled. When you honor yourself, you become who you were meant to be. It takes courage to do this.

After the tear-stained mid-year review with Geoff, I did what he instructed. I squelched myself. I shrunk. I did not participate in meetings. Instead, I wrote my first book (never published but turned into articles). I sat in the corner and scribbled in a notebook during meetings. It appeared as if I was engaged and being studious, but it was a disengagement technique. I had to disengage because if I listened, I wanted to contribute, to discuss, and understand. I wanted to join the discussion, but it was better for my career, at this firm, to be silent. I rolled into work around nine a.m., took an hour lunch, and a long afternoon walk around the parking lot. I counted the minutes until three thirty when it was acceptable to leave. I did spend more time with my daughter(s), which helped the relocation transition, but at work, I was invisible. Invisible on purpose.

I slowed down the pace of my projects. Instead of three-month project plans, Geoff and I stretched them to nine to twelve-month plans. I informed Geoff that I was working 10-15% of my capacity. I maintained my global level projects but simply drove them at a slower pace. A pace befitting of the division and company where I worked.

It was boring. I was a bad fit for the corporation, or at least that division. I wanted to work, achieve goals, drive productivity, and make a difference. I wanted to be valued and appreciated.

Outwardly I adjusted well. I was silent, furiously taking notes in an inconspicuous seat in each conference room. My year-end review came, and Geoff praised me. He reported how much the leadership liked what I was doing and how successful I was. The perception of me was transformed. I moved the projects at the pace they wanted, I did not offer an opinion, or ask questions. The positive feedback was strange because I felt like I was not working, not delivering.

It felt to me that I was not contributing. During that fall, no projects were completed, because of the long timelines and due dates. I flew around the world gaining consensus on projects, but little was accomplished. It was more planning and talking about doing than actually doing anything. My year-end review was a wild success. Geoff gave me a significant pay raise, big bonus, and a pile of shares. The shares were unexpected because they were not typically given to people with the title I held. They thought I was doing incredible work, and with the renewed favorable view of my performance, he promised my title change was imminent.

Two weeks after my year-end review, I resigned. The new job had the title I wanted, a 38% pay increase, the opportunity to lead a team of sixty-three people, and in an organization that wanted me to contribute, be productive, and to make a difference.

Find your voice. Honor your place in the world. Decide what you want, then go for it.

INTRODUCTION TO JENNIFER PESTIKAS

Jen Pestikas is a type-A super achiever. She always got straight A's and was devastated if a B showed up on her report card(s). Jen set the bar high and strove to check all the boxes in what defined a successful life. Her super achieving nature shaped her career in the corporate world.

After twenty years in corporate, climbing the ladder in financial services from a bank teller to a Senior Vice President in a Chicago land financial institution and doing 'all the right things', Jen's health plummeted. In 2019, her thrusters burnt out, her body stopped functioning, and emotionally, she was a shell of her former self with no passion nor direction.

Jen's time of healing that followed was an arduous journey and a gift. A gift she had to give herself, her husband, children, and her life. She was forced to acknowledge that lives weren't perfect. She did not have to check all life's success boxes, and she did not have to be super woman. For the first time, Jen finally understood what she wanted. Jen knew she wanted to give back to women so they could avoid the traps of overachieving, perfectionism, and not speaking their truth.

Jen has a Master of Business Administration (MBA) from Lake Forest Graduate School of Management, a Bachelor of Arts (BA) from Indiana University and is coaching certified from the Institute for Professional Excellence in Coaching (iPEC).

Jen has developed the Brave Women at Work brand, hosts the Brave Women at Work podcast, and offers coaching services to women who are looking to get to the next level in their careers. You can listen to the Brave Women at Work podcast on Apple, Google, Stitcher, and Spotify. Connect with Jen at www.bravewomenatwork.com or via LinkedIn.

ON FIRE, BACK FROM BURNOUT
Jennifer Pestikas

I rapped my fingers on the steering wheel. My breath came in quick sips. The blue car in front of me was not moving. The light. *What color is the light? Are we supposed to be moving?* Gulping in air, anxiety rose in my chest. *Where am I going?* My eyes skittered across the intersection. We are waiting. We are waiting for the green light. I am going home. I am going home for lunch from my office. My office. My work. My responsibility. Nothing is wrong. *Why do I feel like this?* This is my life. Work, kids, husband. Sickness. Work. Health. Work. Babies. *What is happening to my body? What is happening to me?*

It wasn't immediate. It wasn't always like that. It was a long build to my panic attack in the car. I got pregnant with my first daughter, Charlotte, easily. Just like the overachiever that I was. The pregnancy was easy, and the labor and birth were even easier. Charlotte showed up in the world not only on time, but early at thirty-nine weeks. She was a little trooper just like her mama. I pushed 2 or 3 times, and she was out and in this world. I was so in love.

Three years after Charlotte was born, I had the itch to expand our family. My husband, John, wasn't on board. John took on the parental responsibilities for the first three years of Charlotte's life. I didn't know it at the time, but I suffered from extreme postpartum anxiety and depression after she was born. John and I knew that something was off, but only through the lens of experience did we realize what it was. Doctors talked about postpartum depression; anxiety wasn't discussed. In my self-assessment, I didn't check all the postpartum boxes, so I did not say anything to the doctor or my husband. I wish I would have said something much, much sooner because my second bout of postpartum anxiety was one of the first triggering events for my battle with burnout.

Eventually, John came around and agreed to start trying for a second baby. In my overachiever and perfectionist mind, I thought, 'this will be easy'. I will get pregnant as easily as I did with Charlotte, and our second child will be in the world. Little did I know what the struggle to get pregnant with our second child would be.

Three months after John and I started trying to conceive, we found out we were pregnant. I was excited but scared at the same time. I didn't want a repeat of what happened after Charlotte's birth. I was already thinking of the postpartum anxiety and depression. I knew I was pregnant even before I took a pregnancy test. I just knew. I felt great in the first few weeks of pregnancy and was excited for my first set of scans at the doctor's office. I was overjoyed to see the heartbeat flicker on the monitor.

John and I went to that first doctor's appointment together, five weeks after conceiving. The doctor confirmed the pregnancy and showed us the grainy blip of a heartbeat on the ultrasound monitor. I was ecstatic to be expanding our family. In my mind, I felt like I had the opportunity to do a 'do over' as a mother of an infant. I would not have postpartum anxiety or depression this time. I would be more involved with this new little life. We went home and we were tempted to tell Charlotte, who was four years old at the time, but we decided to wait.

Although John offered to come along to the nine-week appointment, I told him I was comfortable going on my own. I settled into the orderly waiting area for my name to be called. I was calm and enthusiastic to see the baby's heartbeat again. Dr. T., my gynecologist, came into the dark room. After delivering Charlotte, he knew me and my personality. He knew how to help keep me relaxed. He started the ultrasound and rolled the cool wand over my stomach. I craned my neck around to see the monitor. No heartbeat. Dr. T pushed a bit harder on my stomach and moved the ultrasound wand around and around in different angles, trying to find the flickering blip. Still, no heartbeat. His face fell, and his mouth formed a tight line. He was trying to hide his disappointment. The baby wasn't alive. There was no heartbeat. He said all the right words, this was common, better to lose it now. I could not hear over the thrumming in my ears. He mentioned something about a 'missed miscarriage'. I needed a D&C procedure. I left my body and was hovering above myself. I saw my form on the table. I stared at my horrified face. I re-entered my body and the tears came. I slammed into my clothes, my hand fumbling with the zipper. I stomped into my shoes. A wave to the receptionist was all I managed while racing to my car. I held onto the steering wheel as I turned the ignition and hiccup sobbed.

I have no idea how I drove home from that appointment. I have no recollection of the drive. My shallow breathing prevented my thoughts. I collapsed into John's arms while Charlotte sat snuggled in her post-bath towel. She eyed me warily and fiddled with her toy fish.

The next year was a blur. I felt like a failure because I was confident my second pregnancy was going to be just like my first one. To numb myself out, I worked non-stop. I felt that if I was frozen personally, I could excel professionally. It was unhealthy. Towards the end of the year, I told John that I was finally ready to try again. Before I knew it, I experienced the early signs and symptoms of pregnancy. Heavy breasts and nausea accompanied me each day. I felt a mixture of excitement and fear and decided to keep the potential pregnancy to myself, at least for a while.

One day, I vacuumed mindlessly in our living room as part of my weekly cleaning. I pushed the vacuum across the rug, and a ripping pain shot through my abdomen. I told John I felt sick. I went to bed that evening feeling nauseous and weak but thought I could simply sleep it off.

The next morning, I got ready for work as normal. That morning, I sat in the audience of an all-employee meeting. A cleaving pain slashed my insides. I bent over holding my middle and rushed to the bathroom and put my head in the toilet. Nothing. I didn't throw up. The searing pain did not relent. I splashed water on my face and gripped the edges of the sink. *What is wrong with me?* I had an impending dread. I knew something was wrong. I had to go to the doctor, immediately.

I called John on the way and told him what was happening. The internist got me in, and I described the deep pains and nausea. He asked if I was pregnant. I told him that I wasn't sure. They did two pregnancy tests to confirm the status. The doctor swept into the room and breathlessly told me that I was indeed pregnant. I was happy but also fearful of the stabbing pain that was growing by the minute. The doctor had me lie back on the sterile examination table and felt my abdomen for a few minutes. As the doctor pressed on my stomach, the pain became unbearable. I turned from him to escape the agony. The doctor told me that he was afraid I was having an ectopic pregnancy.

I had to go to the ER immediately. I could barely walk, but I managed to shuffle to the car and gingerly lowered myself into the seat. The pain was explosive and made seeing difficult. The deep breaths to calm me were not working even as I called John to let him know I was going to the hospital. This was not my first in-the-car trauma, and it would not be my last. When I arrived at the hospital, I inched my way through the doors. The woman at check-in saw my pale and sweaty face and directed me to sit in the waiting room. John hurried in minutes later, and I was rushed off to get an ultrasound. I watched with trepidation the scans and the ultrasound tech's face, but nothing. A moment later, the doctor came into the room with a solemn face and gave me the news: I was having an ectopic pregnancy and needed emergency surgery.

Doctors and nurses scurried around me and raced my bed down the long, ugly taupe hall to surgery prep. I was having an ovarian ectopic pregnancy, which happens in only 3% of ectopic pregnancies. There was a liter of blood in my abdomen, and the bleeding continued. They had to save my life. In doing so, they would terminate the pregnancy; of course, babies don't grow and develop in an ovary. The doctor was a miracle worker. He saved my ovary. He saved me from bleeding to death internally. He saved my life. If I had gone to bed that night without going to the hospital, I would not have woken up.

I was grateful to be alive and yet I was an empty shell. A hole in my womb matched the hole in my psyche. I stared into space wondering what was wrong with me. Who was I? Why couldn't I carry a baby? I was uncomfortable in my skin and at war with my body and mind. I couldn't wait to get back to work; I didn't want to be alone with myself or the memories. I didn't want to feel. I just wanted to numb out again. I wanted to escape. It worked before; it could work again.

After the days and months passed, John and I decided to pursue in-vitro fertilization (IVF) to get pregnant. Well, not John. It was more of my decision, and eventually John came along. As my world unraveled and work didn't cover my escape as it had before, I felt a sense of urgency to control the situation. Anything to get my life and work back in order. Up until that point, I methodically controlled every detail of my life. Why not control having a second baby?

Things got real with IVF when the drugs and needles arrived in the mail. It's unnerving to open a box that will consume your life for the next month, if not several months. I pushed work to the side while I was more focused on the timing of shots and unending doctors' appointments. I felt overwhelming anxiety and pressure as I held my breath and impatiently waited for results between appointments. I hoped and prayed for a positive pregnancy.

I was one of the lucky ones. At thirty-nine years old, my embryo implantation resulted in a viable pregnancy. Did I slow down and enjoy the pregnancy and my upcoming rainbow baby? Of course not. I didn't take a moment to stop and appreciate that my body was growing an amazing life. I was too scared and disconnected to allow myself any time for preparation. At the end of the harrowing experience, my rainbow baby, Olivia, arrived on a sunny June day. Olivia has been a such a bright spot in our lives and one that I'm happy we fought for.

After these experiences of loss, you think that I would have changed my perspective on work. I didn't. I used work as my diversion. Escape from the pain. Distract me from the sadness and worries that I was not good enough, or something was wrong with me. While pregnant with Olivia, my work-life was demanding. I was responsible for every inch of the brand merchandising for a new 30,000 square foot office space. I am, or was, a perfectionist. I lead fearlessly and without pause. There was momentous weight on me and my team, everything had to be perfect for the grand opening. I went from office to office and conference room to conference room to check every sign, every wall and piece of artwork. I walked the 30,000 square foot facility several times over and over, confirming everything was ready and exactly perfect. I ignored the signs of exhaustion.

I had a new baby and a demanding career. The first crack in my facade was the day I broke down in tears in front of my team. It was not a well-up and tearful delivery; it was open sobbing in front of everyone. This was not how I worked. This was not me. I couldn't hold it in anymore; my anguish was pushing through the walls I had so carefully built. I left early that day to compose myself. My body's alarm bells were blaring, and I continued to shove the signs away. I didn't listen. I didn't listen to myself. In June, the grand opening was perfect, and minus the one crying episode, no one noticed I was unraveling. Not even me.

By January of the following year, I had more physical symptoms of stress and burnout. My skin was suddenly turning red. I had rosacea and had never had it before. I had new stomach issues and problems eating. My allergy symptoms were exploding. And if that wasn't enough, as the avalanche of other signs and symptoms was just beginning; insomnia snaked its way into my nights. I never had problems with sleep before, and now I could not sleep. I awoke at three a.m. every night. I could not fall back asleep. I beat myself up at night. *Why couldn't I sleep? What is wrong with me?* Lack of sleep is devastating and frustrating. It caused me to feel crazy and emotionally unhinged. After the insomnia kicked in, then came the anxiety and depression. This round of anxiety and depression was different than my postpartum anxiety with Charlotte. Escaping into work and my other tried and true numbing behaviors weren't working. The anxiety was crippling. I was unsafe in my body because I didn't know what was happening to me. I ran to a bevy of doctors only to discover each doctor treated only the symptoms within their specialty. The dermatologist tried to help my skin but didn't address nor ask about my other issues. My internist tried to help with my digestion but didn't address my skin.

I worked on, killer hours and high stress, and by the following fall, my symptoms couldn't be ignored. The panic attacks came on fast and furious. I was out of control. And then the scariest symptom of all appeared: hair loss. At first, I noticed that I was shedding more than normal. Even though it had been a year since I had Olivia, I thought it was related to giving birth. My hair fell out in larger and larger quantities. I went to the doctor to get tested for everything under the sun. Iron levels, vitamin levels, thyroid, hormones, SIBO, parasites, adrenal fatigue, signs of cancer. You name it, I was tested for it. No solution or root cause was found. Each morning, the shower was my enemy. A tentative step into the tiled space caused my heart to race and my breath to catch. Globs of hair on the floor, sticking to my chest, awaited me when I reached for my robe. I didn't realize nor appreciate the trauma of losing hair until it happened every day. My hair continued to fall out because the pressure at work remained high. My husband also struggled with a long-term illness that prevented him from being able to help, even though he tried. The challenges were coming from all sides, and it became too much.

I knew I needed a break. A lunch break at home might help. I was unprepared for the blossom of panic in the car. The panic attack was fierce.

The anxiety completely enveloped me, and I couldn't breathe. I am not sure how I got home. I threw my car into park and rushed into the house. I gripped the edge of the kitchen counter and bent in half, gasping for air. My husband, John, ran downstairs. He asked what was wrong with me, but I couldn't talk. Each breath felt like life or death. He was scared. I saw it in his eyes. He told me that I couldn't go back to work. *I told him I had to.* My perfectionism and people-pleasing grew to such a fever pitch that they clouded the obvious. I needed a break. I needed time away from work. I completely unraveled and couldn't take one more step. John had to call my boss. He told him about my panic attack and that I needed time off work.

Behind the fear in his eyes, I could see a deeper concern, a knowledge. He wanted to call the hospital. My heart caught in my chest, and I felt more panic race into my veins. "Why?" I asked him. "Why do I need to call the hospital?" He explained that the hospital had outpatient mental health facilities. Anger replaced the panic. I didn't need a hospital! *What I needed was to go back to work!* He tried to calm me down, and the deep breaths slowed my pulse. I dialed the number and talked with the hospital's patient enrollment coordinator. I was confused, frustrated, and afraid. They wanted to evaluate me. I did not want to go. How else was I going to beat the crippling fear and the black dot of anxiety that now defined my life? I went.

At the hospital, I cautiously filled out the mental health form. The form asked scary questions like "Do you struggle getting out of bed?" and "Have you lost pleasure in things?" I was tempted to lie to ace the test, but I didn't. When I looked at my results, they were confirmation I needed help. *I needed help.* That was the first time admitting to myself that I couldn't do this on my own. The way I was living my life was not sustainable. I couldn't hide behind work or achievements anymore. I could not numb myself with an avalanche of assignments. The doctor diagnosed me with clinical depression and anxiety.

For the next three months, I made the daily trek to an outpatient hospital program for people struggling to cope with their mental health issues. It was humbling. I never thought I would get to that point, but there I was, learning ways to handle my stress, depression, and anxiety. Escaping into work was not coping, it was hiding. I went to therapy and shared my patterns of overwork and need for achievement to prove I was enough. I recorded my thoughts in a daily journal, took medication, prayed, and learned to meditate.

As more time passed, I grew worried what people at the office might think of me. Would they think I was a failure? Would they think I wasn't enough? Did they wonder why I disappeared? Through my healing, I realized my health issues overrode my insecurities. I knew that if I kept overworking myself, I would be on a dangerous path to more severe health problems. I had pushed my body to keep going until it couldn't anymore. I hit a wall after burying my symptoms for years upon years.

Burnout is confusing because my hard work was always rewarded with success. I was the student who got straight A's. I was the employee who was promoted and climbed the corporate ladder. I was the family member and friend that everyone turned to for support. Burnout has been a unique type of reckoning because the behaviors and attitudes that led to my success no longer worked. I was forced to admit that I couldn't do it all and attempt to be all things to all people. I've had to discover new ways of being in the world and showing up in my workplace and community.

A key realization through this period of healing was that my identity is not tied to my accomplishments. I don't need to collect more degrees, letters behind my name, or promotions to prove my worth. I am inherently valuable as I am. I am worthy. I am valuable. While I like to accomplish goals, my accomplishments no longer define me. I am still working on this. This wasn't a decision I made in a day and flipped a switch. These are truths I must continue to remind myself. And I have to commit to these lessons and relearn them when necessary.

In addition, I learned I didn't need to contort myself to fit in. One way that I morphed myself to get ahead in my career was to be more masculine. No acting prissy or high maintenance. I renounced my femininity and camouflaged myself in a man's world. At one point, I blended in so much with "the boys" at work that one of my colleagues told me, "Pestikas, working with you is like working with a dude." At the time, I took pride in his comment. Looking back, I am sad that I created that persona. I realize that I can have a dominant, masculine side and a softer, creative feminine side. These sides of me can co-exist in harmony. Further, I believe that one of the reasons my body broke down is because I operated out of the natural order of who I am. By honoring the light of creativity, intuition, and being heartful, I am now more whole and happier than I have been in years, maybe ever.

How long has it taken me to recover from burnout? I wish I could say that I was 100% after the three months

I took off work, but honestly, I'm still recovering. For me, burnout has been a dance with the devil. Almost an addiction. I have my self-care protocol in place, including continuing my medication, therapy, meditation, and prayer, but I need to be vigilant. If I'm not careful, I can slip into old behavior patterns of overwork and hustling for my worth. If there is a positive aspect to this experience, it's that I know when my body needs a break. I recognize the stress rising in a way that I didn't before. I rest when needed because I don't want to return to the place of fear and panic. I won't let myself return there.

One of the key areas I'm continually working on is boundaries. Saying no sounds easy, but it's not for a recovering perfectionist and people pleaser. I used to override my needs in favor of the needs of my job or others. I put me and my family second. No more. It's still difficult, but I give myself more time to determine if I really want to do something or if it's urgent. As they say, "If it's not a hell yes, it's a no." I'm working hard to get the "hell no's" out of my life.

A few other useful techniques I've adopted to prevent another bout with burnout are meditation, prayer, and body scanning. The first, meditation, is a practice that I thought was out of my reach. When I started meditating, my thoughts would bounce around my head like popcorn, completely out of control. Initially, I got frustrated and decided that meditation was out of my grasp. When I started having radical compassion for my racing mind, I could relax into meditation. I experienced fleeting moments of tranquility. With time, I've had more peace and self-awareness. Meditation has made an enormous difference in my life.

The second, prayer, has been a great teacher to me. As a Christian, prayer has reminded me that I am not in control. By giving up control to God, I have loosened my grip and allowed more space for uncertainty and grace. In turn, this has given me more happiness. Honestly, I can fall into unhealthy habits and try to control everything in times of stress, but now I have prayer as a wonderful practice to lean on.

My final technique is body scanning or checking in with how I'm feeling. With body scanning, I tune into to my body's signs and signals. I've picked up chronic illnesses during this journey, and as hard as it is to admit, my health would probably be in a better place today if I paid attention earlier. When I feel the effects of stress, I make sure to go for a walk, call a friend, or take a break from my laptop. If that's not possible, I take a few deep breaths to be present in my body in that moment. That can be feeling the chair as I'm sitting in it in a meeting or rubbing the ridges of my fingerprints to be mindful of the moment. These small habits have paid huge dividends.

If my story resonates with you, I encourage you to check-in with yourself. Have you been overworking for a long time? Do you ignore your physical, mental, or emotional symptoms out of a need to achieve, please, perfect, or perform? If so, take a moment to reflect on my journey and take it as a cautionary tale. Don't let yourself get so far that you experience burnout. You can turn your professional and personal life around before it spins out of control. Maybe I needed to hit the wall of burnout to really get the message. Who knows? What I am sure of is that I would not wish that on anyone. I hope my story encourages you to take care of yourself, to set boundaries, and to honor your heart. You don't need to hustle to prove your worth. You don't need to contort yourself to fit in. You are you. You are valuable. You are worthy, just as you are.

EPILOGUE

While reading, editing, re-reading, and re-editing this work, several themes revealed themselves. The strength and resilience of women is real. The willingness, capability, and eagerness to strive, to be successful, to find joy, drive women to overcome incredible challenges.

Women's identity and self-worth are commonly tied to their ability to have children, the challenges with childbearing and childrearing. Would men's stories of perseverance be this intricately linked to fatherhood? I surmise that they would not. The physical, mental, and emotional burden (and joys) of childbearing is a significant component of a woman's life. This is a simple truth that we must acknowledge.

Women's success is often linked to their ability to hide their mental, physical, or emotional challenges or to camouflage themselves in the workplace. These stories show that when we hide ourselves we are serving no one, including ourselves. We each have a battle to fight, and the colleague next to you may be experiencing a life-changing situation that you know nothing about. Giving people a measure of grace, including ourselves, goes a long way in making this world a better place.

It is important to create space for reflection and planning. Meditation, focusing on goals, and prayer techniques were deployed by our authors. After this period of reflection, the authors rose to the challenge and persevered. Then they put pen to paper, wrote, and worked their plans. The act of writing and taking action were instrumental in their personal and professional achievements.

Finally, the authors illustrated that finding your voice and being true to yourself is the path to transformation. When people embrace their full selves, their joy and power are unmatched. Remember, you are exactly who are meant to be, so embrace who you are and lean into your identity.

We are honored to share the stories of these women and their resilience. We are hopeful that within these pages you found inspiration, motivation, and guidance. Guidance that helps you to your own transformation and growth.

Find your voice. Honor your place in the world. Decide what you want, then go for it.

DISCUSSION GUIDE

First, Only, Different

1. This chapter highlights several key strategies (i.e., wellness practices, leaning on a support network, reconnecting to core values, pushing through fear, etc.) for navigating challenging times. What stands out that you can incorporate into your toolbox?
2. Being first, only, or different can add unintended stress and pressure to team members. As a leader or manager, what lessons can you take from the author's story to create a more inclusive and supportive space for all team members--particularly FODs?
3. The author shares that reconnecting to her values was essential to leading in challenging times. What core values serve as guideposts for you and why?

4. Political, environmental, and external factors can heighten workplace pressures and employee performance. What ideas do you have for keeping a finger on the pulse on how this these factors might be impacting the team?

Reinvention or Defeat?

1. Describe a time when you were at the intersection of Reinvention and Defeat? How did you navigate it?
2. Which of the seven steps in the outlined reinvention process resonated with you?
3. The author was faced with a significant personal event that was intrinsically linked to her professional life and financial well-being. What techniques did she deploy to navigate that? What might you have done differently?
4. Who can you assemble to help you get out of your comfort zone to boldly embrace your next reinvention?

What did I read?

1. Sometimes we don't know who helped us, nudged us, or provided the spark of inspiration for moving us forward until we're looking in the rearview mirror. Looking back, who has helped you over a significant challenge that you did not recognize at that time?

2. When has fear of the future kept you from pursuing what you wanted to do? How much of that fear is still present in your life today? What might you do about it now?
3. How do you know when you need to lean on others for support or strength?
4. Knowing that people live everyday with all kinds of challenges (including you), what would you like the office-place to do differently to acknowledge, include, or support others in the workplace? What part might you play in making that happen?

My Own Two Feet

1. Immigration stories are often terrifying and powerful. Would you be willing to upend your life to live in a new country? What inspiring immigration stories do you have to share?
2. How do you feel about both partners financially contributing? How important is financial independence and capability to you?
3. The author showed great strength and focus on raising her children. What can we learn from that focus? What might you have done the same or differently?

Staying Power: Thriving in the Storm

1. What affirmations do you have in your life? Do you have a mantra to help you achieve positive outcomes?
2. How do you demonstrate vulnerability? How do you manage your mental well-being?
3. How are you learning to T.H.R.I.V.E.?

Wolf Bites

1. How did you feel after reading this deeply personal story?
2. Have you known or suspected someone at work struggling with a significant health issue? How did you or could you help them?
3. What advice might you give a colleague with a health condition after reading this chapter?

Only Speak When Spoken To

1. Do you notice yourself diminishing your contribution? What examples can you share?
2. What could the author have done differently in her experience and still be successful? Do you think she responded appropriately?
3. What can you do to reduce the times you, or your team members or colleagues, diminish themselves or their contributions?

Back From Burn Out

1. Have you ever overworked despite an illness, injury, or loss? What was the outcome? How did it impact you?
2. Think of a time you struggled to say no or hold your boundaries personally or professionally. What was the outcome?
3. Have you personally experienced burnout? If so, what happened and how did you heal? If you haven't, what are some of the signs you should be looking for in times of high stress?
4. What are some ways that you take care of yourself in busy seasons?

ACKNOWLEDGEMENT
Jennifer Pestikas

I would like to start by thanking Hope Mueller, who listened to my crazy idea to write this book. Little did I know the amazing journey that we would travel together over the past twelve months. Hope has been an amazing teacher, mentor, and friend. I look forward to partnering with Hope on many projects in the years to come.

Thank you, Tiffany Harelik, of Spellbound Press, for helping us launch this book and get it into the world. Your guidance, insight, and feedback have been invaluable to me personally and professionally.

Thank you to the contributing authors for their passion and dedication to the book process.

Thank you, Alison Martin, Founder and Managing Director of Engage Mentoring, for being the first person to sponsor an author for this book. Your early support and encouragement mean the world to me.

To the readers, followers, and members of the Brave Women at Work community, your willingness to participate in this growing group of amazing women is awe-inspiring. I am grateful for you, and it is for you that I do this work.

I would like to thank my beautiful daughters, Charlotte and Olivia Pestikas. Charlotte, you forever changed my world in the most wonderful way when I became your mama. Olivia, thank you for the joy and light you bring to our lives. You remind me to appreciate each moment of love and laughter we share together.

A big thank you to my niece, Abby Lemon. Abby was an early Brave Women at Work podcast listener and encouraged the writing of this book. I love you, Abby, and want you to know you can do anything you put your heart and mind to.

To my mom, Gail Lemon. You have been one of my biggest cheerleaders and counselors throughout my career. Thank you for always giving it to me straight and loving me through it all.

And to my husband, John Pestikas. I appreciate your support and encouragement of my dream to help women get the education and inspiration they need to take braver and bolder action in their careers. I love you!

ACKNOWLEDGEMENT
Hope Mueller

First, I must acknowledge Jennifer Pestikas, who without hesitation, jumped into this project with me. She coined the phrase 'naïve joy' and we rushed headlong into, what I suspect will be, a lifelong partnership. She is an amazing partner, unparalleled in her commitment and drive, and a pure joy to work with.

Tiffany Harelik, of Spellbound Press, continues to be the rockstar operator, deploying her now familiar brand of bracing honesty and focused cheerleading.

The contributing authors must be recognized. They were willing partners on our 'naïve joy' journey and they too never wavered in their commitment to the project.

Big thank you to my dedicated readers, followers, and subscribers. Their willingness to purchase, share, like, post, and help promote does not go unnoticed and without whom all projects would be abject failures. The list is too long to include but please know that I see and appreciate you.

My four daughters who all show more confidence and aplomb than I at their respective ages. They bring me more joy and pride than could be imagined or adequately described.

Thank you to my mom, Paula Cordes, for your unconditional love which laid the foundation for every measure of success I achieve and enjoy today.

Thank you, Brad Mueller. Your steadfast love and acceptance of me, and generous support of these projects, is the center of my universe. You are the best thing that ever happened to me. Let's do this!

CPSIA information can be obtained
at www.ICGtesting.com
Printed in the USA
BVHW091133071022
648919BV00016B/777/J